Walking Through the Shadows

The year after

by Karen Todd Scarpulla

Little White Dog Press

PUBLISHED BY LITTLE WHITE DOG PRESS

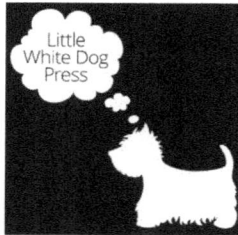

ISBN-10: 0989158950
ISBN-13: 978-0-9891589-5-4

First Edition

This book is dedicated to my parents Jim and Marilyn.

To my father, who passed away in June 2013, I thank you for instilling in me your creative and entrepreneurial spirit.

To my mother, the strongest woman I know, who is learning to navigate life without my father after fifty years of marriage, thank you for always standing by my side and encouraging me to be a writer.

TABLE OF CONTENTS

INTRODUCTION

In 2012, I experienced the most challenging year of my life. I found myself standing at a fork in the road and about to embark on a path littered with rocks and ruts. I knew the road would be bumpy, but I had no idea just how much the journey would change everything.

In December of 2011, I made the choice to move my children and myself back in with my ex-husband so they could spend quality time with their father, who had terminal cancer. We had been divorced for six years and were not friends. In fact, I was counting down the days until the children were in college so that Vince and I would no longer have to communicate on a regular basis. We could barely speak to one another without our dislike penetrating our dialogue. Our divorce had been quick, but it was filled with rage and bitterness—like most other divorces, I suppose. Choosing to share the same roof with someone whom I had tried so hard to distance myself from was not a decision to take lightly. Not only would I be living with Vince again, but I would also be taking care of him as his health deteriorated. Events had unfolded so quickly, however, that it seemed the universe really wanted me to take that rocky, twisted, rutted, messed-up path.

As part of our divorce settlement, I had remained in the house we had lived in while married so that the children would not have to be uprooted from their neighborhood, school and life. Little did I know that the housing market would tank, and I would lose all the equity in the house, which was my nest egg. The cost of maintaining a large residence had proven difficult, so in 2008, I had put our house on the market. After three years, I finally received an offer the same night Vince called to tell me he had cancer. I knew this was the universe sending me a sign.

Our children were teenagers. I knew it would be very stressful for them to split their time between our homes. James was preparing to leave for college. Kate was in her junior year of high school; she was very busy scheduling university visits, maintaining her grades and taking entrance exams. And now their dad had cancer. I knew both James and Kate would want to spend as much time as possible with their father and care for him. Timing is everything. Had the children been younger, I would never have suggested we all live together.

I love my children more than words can convey. I make every decision with their needs in mind. Vince had been a very detached father, and I wanted James and Kate to have the opportunity to know him before he passed. Suddenly, time was a luxury, a commodity not to be wasted any longer.

People are shocked at my decision to move back in with my ex, and most tell me that there is no way they could or would make the same sacrifice. The ten months we lived together were pretty crazy—and even awful at times—but I would do it all over again. You can read the complete story of those days in my first book, *Walking Toward the Light: A journey in forgiveness and death.*

Our children have now made it through the first year since their father's passing and are happy and healthy creating their own lives. They have accepted his death and celebrate the time we had with him. This book provides an intimate snapshot of how each of us navigated our grief. I reflect on many of the decisions we made for Vince's care before he passed. We were not prepared for the sacrifices required of a family when planning for a loved one to die at home. With more healthcare options available, many families are making the same choice to help terminally ill patients spend their last months or days at home. It's a trend that I advocate. But with cancer and death come fear. I hope that this book helps remove the fear of the unknown and what to expect. I want to share our story so that others can better prepare to care for terminally ill family members and embrace the time they have left together.

Our legacy is the shadows we leave behind for our loved ones and friends. In this book, I provide a month-by-month chronicle of how each of us walked through the shadows Vince left for us and how we encountered him in the months after his death. We were fortunate that we had time with him. I share with you what we did to prepare the family for his death and how we managed our grief and embraced the future. There are also things I caution you to avoid and things I wish we had done differently.

Death happens. It is a natural part of the circle of life. By demystifying the process of death, I hope families will feel empowered to accept this transition when the time comes.

CHAPTER ONE

SEPTEMBER — PEACE

"The oldest and strongest emotion of mankind is fear, and the oldest and strongest kind of fear is fear of the unknown."
— H.P. Lovecraft

I step back. The white minivan carrying my ex-husband's body slowly pulls out of the driveway. I made Vince a promise. I would be with him until the very end, and that includes watching as the men from the funeral home drive away. Vince is gone. The journey is over. My feet are stuck to the pavement. As the van turns the corner, I dissolve into a puddle of tears. A tidal wave of emotion rushes over me—grief, gratitude and relief. Our journey is over. Or is it just beginning? My family has spent ten months preparing for this day, but it feels as if it has happened too quickly.

For a moment, I have lost all sense of purpose and don't know what to do next. My entire life the last few months has centered on Vince and my children. I feel numb and empty, yet tears continue to pour from my eyes.

"Thank you. Thank you. Thank you," I whisper. A month earlier, fear of this moment pervaded my thoughts every day. I was so afraid that Vince's passing would be traumatic and that he might drown in his own blood.

Many weeks ago I decided we could no longer worry about what was going to happen. My anxiety was stealing my energy. The reality was that his passing would be completely out of our control. One morning, I finally surrendered and trusted that the universe had a plan. I had faith we would be equipped to handle anything that happened. Plans A, B and C were no longer required, and I embraced the notion that we possessed everything we would need. Vince passed gently. And that was our reward for surrendering and letting go of our fear. At 4:50 a.m. on Saturday, September 15th, 2012, he simply went to sleep.

Despite the sadness of the moment, I feel a warm glow and look up at the sky. Why is it that when we want to thank God or the universe we look upwards? My heart swells with gratitude knowing Vince passed peacefully and that he had the opportunity to live with his children again for ten months.

I whisper one last time, "Thank you." I compose myself and head inside to begin the transition.

Vince's mother is sitting at the kitchen table. I know her grief must be deep. She is perfectly put together, dressed, hair done, makeup on—a mask that hides her despair. I, on the other hand, look like a hot mess in leggings, a T-shirt, sneakers and a ponytail. I run my tongue over my teeth. I'm not sure if I even remembered to brush them during all the morning chaos.

"Why did he have to die?" she asks me. "Why didn't God take me?"

God has taken another family member from her. She unexpectedly lost her husband thirteen years earlier after knee surgery complications. She is a staunch Catholic and has spent the last four weeks attending mass daily and praying the rosary every morning in search of a miracle for Vince.

We both played different roles during Vince's illness. She was his connection to God, praying for more time. I was the caretaker for him and our children. I am exhausted, and I don't know the right words to comfort her. What do you say to a mother who has lost her child?

"I'm so sorry. Sometimes it is hard to accept God's plans for us," I say.

A river of tears runs down her face, and I feel absolutely useless.

The doorbell rings. My neighbor has come to walk our dog, Murphy, and deliver a basket of breakfast pastries, juice and flowers. I had texted her earlier to ask for her help. Our neighbors have been so supportive. They've cooked meals, helped with the dog and brought groceries.

I can't stress enough how important it is during the last phases of caring for someone terminally ill to let people help you. Even the smallest of tasks involved in running a household become daunting as you transition to full-time caregiver.

With Murphy on his walk, my thoughts turn to James and Kate, our children. James is planning to drive home from college this morning. I called him last night to tell him hospice warned us that his father would pass this weekend. My heart is so heavy knowing that I must share this news with him over the phone. James left for his first year of college just three weeks earlier. Vince and I both wanted him to start school and get on with his life, no matter what condition Vince was in. I think it gave Vince great comfort to know that his son was beginning his freshman year. I know deep down inside he is very proud of James, even though Vince had a tough time expressing it to him.

I pick up my phone and my heart begins racing.

"Hello."

James' voice is deep, that of a man, and just the sound of it brings a lump to my throat.

"Hey, buddy, I have bad news. Your dad passed away this morning."

"I thought that might happen. How's Nana?"

"She's holding up as well as can be expected. I wanted you to know before you left to drive home this morning. Do you still want to come home?"

He hesitates. "I'm not sure. Do you need me to come home?"

"No. There is really nothing for you to do. But you can certainly come home if you want to."

He hesitates once again. "Can I think about it and call you back? I may just want to stay at school and come home for the funeral." His voice begins to crack. "I'll call you in an hour."

"That's fine. Whatever you want to do—I support you."

I think we are both afraid that if he comes home and takes time off from college, it will be difficult for him to go back. I know that James has supportive friends at school and is doing well in his routine.

Ultimately, when he calls back, he informs me he'd like to remain on campus. I support him in his decision. I truly believe it is for the best. At this point I am focused on what is the right thing for my children.

Vince and I had discussed the importance of the children maintaining their normal lives—or as normal as possible—during his illness and after his death. As a family, we have been grieving Vince's passing and preparing for this moment for ten months. The reality is that after someone close to you dies, life for everyone else moves on. I feel as if I have been running at top speed on a treadmill and someone has hit the stop button and I've been thrown off—but life keeps running along for everyone else. I understand James' desire to get back on the treadmill and restart it as best he can.

Kate is in Philadelphia overnight—where much of Vince's family lives. Vince's cousin had performed an otoplasty on her over the summer, and she needed to have a post-op checkup. Kate is flying home this afternoon. I did not want to share the news with her before she boarded the airplane. The thought of her crying by herself, feeling isolated and alone on the airplane, was too unsettling for me.

With a heavy heart, I call Vince's brother to tell him Vince has passed. He is heartbroken. I ask him not to share the news with his wife or other family members until Kate is on the plane heading to Chicago in just a few hours. She was staying with them. He promises to respect my wishes.

With the most important calls out of the way, my attention turns to organizing the removal of all the medical equipment from the home before Kate arrives. I contact the supply company around nine to confirm they will pick everything up today.

When Vince grew weaker, and we needed to have a medical bed in the last few weeks, I had wanted to put it in the living room. This would have allowed him to watch television all day from bed, the family to gather around him and friends to visit easily. But Vince insisted that the bed be placed in his room upstairs.

"I don't want my bed in the living room," he said. "I don't want me lying in bed dying to be the first thing the kids see each day when they walk into the house. After I am gone, I want them to be able to have friends over without having memories of me dying in the living room."

He had a valid point, so we put the medical bed in his bedroom. As Vince grew weaker, climbing the stairs to his bedroom was difficult. But Vince was adamant that he wanted the children to have as normal an experience living with him as possible.

Choosing where to place a medical bed is a personal decision for family members and needs to be thoroughly discussed. One couple shared a story with me in which the husband was terminally ill. He had insisted the medical bed be placed in the guest room. He did not want to die in the couple's bedroom, where his wife might be left with painful memories.

I appreciate that Vince considered the children's feelings and made the sacrifice to climb the stairs to his room each day until he no longer could. At that point, he began living in his room. This also allowed me to sleep in his regular bed next to the medical bed so I could care for him at night.

Vince was not actually bedridden until the last few days, and I admired his determination to spend time with his friends and family for as long as he could. He climbed the stairs to his room the Tuesday after Labor Day for the last time, just ten days before he passed. Today as I wait for the medical supply company to arrive, I am once again thankful he had the foresight to put the children's needs ahead of his own.

I venture to the kitchen to check in with Vince's mother. She has been quietly sipping a cup of coffee at the table while I have been making calls. I lower myself into the chair across from her. I shift my weight around and fidget. Sitting still is difficult. I am used to keeping busy, running up and down the stairs caring for Vince. Now with him gone and my role of caretaker over, I desperately want something to do, something to distract me from the grief I am beginning to feel.

My mother-in-law breaks the silence. "You should shower and get dressed. People will be coming by today."

The thought of showering and looking pretty today is such a low priority for me, but I realize this will give me something to focus on for a bit. More importantly, I don't want to be disrespectful to my mother-in-law. She has just lost her son, so I do as she has asked. After a quick shower, I again tie my hair back into a ponytail. The thought of blow drying and styling it is more than I can handle. I am pretty sure no one expects us to look beautiful today.

One of my best friends offers to drop by at noon. I am so happy to have this interruption, someone else to break up the silence between my mother-in-law and me.

***

When my friend arrives, we share the story of Vince's passing with her.

"We were so blessed he had such a peaceful passing," I say.

My mother-in-law looks down at the table. "He looked so peaceful, like he just went to sleep."

"The crazy thing is, I think it was really God's plan that he pass last night. Kate is in Philadelphia and it was just the two of us." I look across the table at Vince's mother as I speak.

A lone tear runs down her cheek, and my friend takes her hand.

"Hospice came yesterday," I continue. "And when they found out that I had not slept in four nights, they sent a night nurse. It was a blessing that she was here when he passed. At 2:45 a.m. I heard noise coming from Vince's room, so I got up to check and see if everything was okay. I could see he was agitated. He was grumbling in his sleep, his face was twitching and his hands were moving." A lump catches in my throat as my feelings of sadness come flooding back.

"I asked the nurse what was going on. It's silly. Even though we weren't married any longer, I felt very protective of him."

My friend nods a reassuring smile to me to continue.

"The nurse told me that he had an accident and she had just finished changing his sheets. I was so upset that he was distressed. I sat down on the bed next to him and began rubbing his arm. Murphy was sleeping in Vince's bed still. You know he stayed with Vince the entire night until he passed?"

My friend offers another smile. "I'm not surprised. Murphy has a big heart."

Vince's mother's face softens for a moment. "I tried to make him leave when I went to bed, but he growled at me."

I take a deep breath and continue. "I began rubbing his arm, trying to comfort him and calm him down. I didn't think he was dying. In fact, I really didn't think he would pass until later in the weekend.

I kept rubbing his arm and assuring him that everything was going to be okay. I kept telling him to calm down and to try to get some sleep. I told him to stop worrying and that I would take care of James and Kate. I rubbed his arm for about thirty minutes until he seemed to be resting comfortably. I bent down and gave him a kiss on his forehead and told him to get some sleep and that I would see him in the morning." My voice cracks at this point in the story.

My friend reaches over and places her other hand on top of mine.

"Once he was calm," I continue, "I headed back down to my room. I was wide awake by then, so I decided to try to get some work done. It was so weird. About ten minutes later, Murphy jumped off Vince's bed and went to lay in his dog bed in the hallway right outside my bedroom door. I left my bedroom door open so I could hear the nurse. I called Murphy to come into my room, but he refused to move from the hallway. It seemed just like a few minutes later the nurse appeared in my door and told me that Vince had passed. I have to tell you I was shocked. The first word out of my mouth was, 'no!' I ran down to his room, and there was a beautiful yellow glow around his bed. He looked so peaceful. I immediately put my hand on his chest to make sure the nurse did not make a mistake."

My mother-in-law looks up at me. "I knew when Karen turned on the light in my room that he had passed."

"I am so grateful we had a nurse last night," I say. "She immediately called hospice who sent another nurse over to help with all the arrangements."

Tears stream down my friend's face as I finish my story.

What I don't share with my friend and Vince's mother is the overwhelming guilt I am experiencing for not staying with him last night. I am angry with myself for leaving his side. He must have been passing as I sat with him rubbing his arm. I wonder if that is why he became calm. Had he died then?

My friend asks if we would like to pray together. I appreciate that she knows how comforting this will be for my mother-in-law. We all hold hands.

"We give thanks for Vince's peaceful passing," she says, "and that he is with God and no longer in pain."

Vince's mother adds, "And bless Karen, who cared for Vince until the very end."

I appreciate this moment of recognition from Vince's mother. She and I had always been very close, and the last few weeks had been hard for both of us while we assumed roles we never fathomed we would be asked to fulfill.

We sit for a while longer before I break the silence. "Kate will arrive home this afternoon, and I am hoping all the medical equipment is gone before she gets here."

My friend asks if she can help me tidy up Vince's room and put it back together the way it was before he got sick. "It might be nice for Kate not to be reminded of his illness."

We head upstairs, and I suddenly realize just how many medical supplies we have. We begin disposing of everything. I am grateful for her help. Even though I knew Vince was gone, I was worried it would be disrespectful to dispose of his toiletries.

But who is going to want his toothbrush?

I encourage everyone going through a similar situation to allow friends to help you with the cleaning up process. They bring a helpful outside perspective.

We finish removing five trash bags of supplies from Vince's room, and the medical supply company arrives. They take the last of the reminders of Vince's illness away. Somehow having all the equipment removed from the house allows us to turn our attention to remembering happier and funnier times with Vince. As my best friend leaves, Vince's best friend arrives and several more of my friends join us. In honor of Vince, we decide to make cocktails and toast his passing. My mother-in-law, who rarely has a glass of wine, even enjoys a cocktail, as well. We sip our drinks and share funny stories of Vince. More friends join us throughout the afternoon, and we continue celebrating Vince's life. Even his mother is able to experience a break from her sadness by sharing humorous stories of Vince as a child.

"I have to pick Kate up from the airport," I say.

"Let me drive you," Vince's friend offers.

***

Vince's friend has a convertible, and the wind feels great on my face. Kate sends a text. She is waiting at the curb in the arrivals area. We pull up, and I quickly step out of the car.

She knows as soon as she sees us. "Is he gone?"

"Yes. I am so sorry." I grab her and hug her tightly. "Are you okay?" I ask.

"Yeah, I knew he was going to die before I got home."

Thursday night before she left, Kate and I took a walk, and I explained to her that her father was growing weaker and he may pass over the weekend. I asked her how she would feel if he passed while she was gone.

She answered with wisdom beyond her age. "I think there is a reason I have to fly to Philadelphia tomorrow. Maybe I'm not supposed to be here when it happens."

On our way home from the airport, I receive a phone call from one of Vince's cousins. After sharing his condolences, he lets me know that my sister-in-law is not pleased with me.

"You have put her in a horrible position having to lie to Kate all day," he says.

Apparently, Vince's brother did tell his wife, and she was angry she could not tell Kate the news herself. She did not appreciate having to lie. This news is so upsetting to me. I am emotionally and physically exhausted from months of caring for Vince. My nerves are exposed. Anger begins to bubble up inside of me. I don't need the additional family drama right now.

I know I need to separate myself from the family dynamics that will arise over the next few days, weeks and months. In the face of grief, people develop their own agendas, and those who like drama will find a way to create it.

When a family member dies, choosing not to engage in the drama of others is often easier said than done. Each family member will handle the news of a death in his or her own way and want to grieve in his or her own way. Some family members will want to place blame, some will withdraw and some will be angry.

I am grateful that before Vince passed, he and I discussed the need for the children's grief and wishes to be put first. After getting off the phone with Vince's cousin, I vow to make James' and Kate's emotional well-being my compass at all times—no matter what arises with family dynamics. This is a life-changing event for them. Helping them adjust to life without their father is my priority. James, Kate and I will walk through the legacy of Vince's shadows together as a united front.

CHAPTER TWO

OCTOBER — A CELEBRATION

"To pretend angels do not exist because they are invisible is to believe we never sleep because we don't see ourselves sleeping."
—Thomas Aquinas

I have always viewed funerals and memorial services as events that help those left behind to grieve. It is an opportunity for friends and family to gather and celebrate the life of the person who has passed. Other people see it as a solemn occasion to mourn the loss. Everyone has his or her own way of dealing with death. Grief is a unique journey for each of us. There is no right or wrong way to grieve, and there is no timeline. During bereavement there should be no judgments—only compassion and empathy for everyone involved. When we are judged for our suffering or sorrow, it creates unnecessary drama and only serves to intensify our anguish.

It was Vince's wish that we have two memorial services, one in Chicago, where we are currently living, and another in Philadelphia, where he grew up. He had taken time to create guest lists for each location and even selected the venues. The children were aghast at the idea of having to endure two memorial services. One memorial service would be painful enough for them. Before Vince had even passed, the children begged me to have just one service.

The funeral director is kind enough to come to our home to help us coordinate all the arrangements. The house is filled with friends, so I suggest we have our meeting on the deck.

"Do you need me?" Vince's mother asks.

"I will need the funeral home information for Philadelphia. It's up to you if you would like to sit with us."

Her grief is fresh, and I know it will be difficult for to hear the arrangements for cremation, but she gathers her notes and sits with us.

The funeral director begins, "I am so sorry for your loss."

"Thank you," we both respond in unison.

She looks at Vince's mother. "I had the chance to meet your son when he came in to make arrangements. I thought it was so kind of him to want everything arranged before he passed."

I remember the day we went to the funeral home together and how depressing it was for both of us. Our visit to the funeral home was confirmation that he was dying. The meeting was emotionally draining, and Vince asked to leave early. His sad appearance was more than I could bear. I had decided when we left that I would encourage Vince to leave the rest of the arrangements to me. Planning your own funeral while having a terminal illness is like accepting defeat. While Vince knew his death was inevitable, a visit to the funeral home was like announcing the cancer had won.

"When would you like the service?" the funeral director asks.

"The children and I have decided to have just one service," I say.

"But Vince wanted two services," his mother says.

"I know, but the children have asked me to have just one. They do not feel strong enough to go through two services. I think it would be best to have one funeral, and it should be in Norristown, Pennsylvania, at your family's church."

I hope that the news that the entire event will take place in her church gives her some comfort. I feel guilty pushing back, but my primary concern at this point is for my children.

Vince's mother sits silently as she absorbs the news and then opens her small address book to retrieve the information for the funeral home in Norristown.

Losing a parent as a teenager is a devastating event. James is only eighteen and Kate sixteen. I am trying to balance James' and Kate's needs while also being supportive and understanding of Vince's mother's loss. Vince has a rather large family in the Philadelphia area, and my thinking is that a service with all of my mother-in-law's family around her to support her will be easier for her. The children will also feel at ease only having to endure one service. Any friends willing to travel to a service in Chicago will have no problem flying to Philadelphia instead. A Philadelphia funeral will allow his family the opportunity to plan a service they feel appropriate at their family church.

Even though the memorial mass and funeral will be held in Pennsylvania, there is still much to coordinate here. The funeral home in Chicago will cremate Vince per his instructions. His ashes will be divided among James, Kate and Vince's mother. Vince's mother's portion will be shipped to the funeral home in Philadelphia that will oversee the burial. Vince's mother's wish is to have his ashes buried in a Catholic cemetery. While the Catholic Church now allows cremation, the remains must be buried in consecrated ground. Vince had wanted his ashes split between James and Kate. He wanted them to spread his ashes somewhere that is meaningful to them, someplace that reminds them of him.

In order to accommodate everyone's wishes, the funeral director has recommended splitting the ashes in half. One half will be given to Vince's mother for burial and the other half will be divided into four equal parts. The children will receive a small bag of ashes to scatter, and a small portion will be sealed in a special memorial vessel for them to keep. I am pleased with this recommendation, because it protects everyone's wishes.

The funeral director also arranges for obituaries to be placed in local newspapers for several cities where Vince has resided. We stand to thank her and say our goodbyes. My mother-in-law's eyes fill with tears as she shakes her hand. The finality of the situation hangs over us. We are all struggling with our grief, including me—much to my surprise.

Several days later, my mother-in-law and I sit at the dining room table composing an email to send to Vince's friends, family and business associates.

"Do you think many people will come to Philadelphia?" she asks.

"Anyone who was willing to fly to Chicago will be willing to fly to Philadelphia," I say. "I have to honor the children's wishes for one memorial service."

"I know. I just want all his friends to be able to come."

"The funeral is over three weeks away. People will have plenty of time to make arrangements. Besides, Vince is gone, and I think it is important that we do what is best for James and Kate right now."

Out of respect for Vince's family, I leave the planning of the service in Philadelphia to them. His mother and his sister-in-law plan everything. I am incredibly grateful not to be involved anymore. I want to focus on James and Kate, and unexpectedly I am dealing with my own set of emotions.

***

As I begin to make plans for our family to travel to Philadelphia, worry creeps into my thoughts. I am already starting to see differences in how each family member is handling his or her grief. The children and I had been experiencing anticipatory grief for months leading up to Vince's death. Our grieving process began the day we accepted the inevitability that Vince would die. So we are further along in the grief process than most of Vince's family members seem to be. This becomes very evident the day I speak with Vince's brother. He calls me to check in on his mother and to tell me that he spoke with James. I immediately thank him. I am grateful that Vince's brother is stepping in to connect with James. He will now be the patriarch for both James and Kate. He will have the responsibility of keeping Vince's family connected to James and Kate throughout their lives, just as Vince requested of him.

"I talked to James yesterday," he begins, "and I am more upset than he is."

His words strike a chord, and I can feel my mother tiger rise up in me. I do not appreciate his judgment of James.

"He said he is staying at school."

"James feels it is best to stay at school and in his routine," I explain. "He offered to come home if I needed help. There is nothing for him to do at home, and his support system is at school. I think it is good he stays in his routine."

Many people expect James and Kate to fall apart, stay home from school for weeks, cancel plans and cry all the time. But James and Kate choose to remain stoic around others and process their heartache in private. They both opt to stick with their normal habits as much as possible.

We currently have a core societal belief that death is bad, and when someone dies, we must be overtly mournful because we have lost someone we loved. We expect people to be embroiled in grief and despair, to wear black and withdraw. However, the familiarity of a routine can be comforting. It forces you to continue moving forward, living. The more you focus on the pain and loss, the more you will become mired in grief and stuck in emotional despair. This can lead to depression if it is not dealt with properly.

Early on while living with Vince, we sat down as a family and accepted what was about to happen. We never gave the children false hope or prayed for miracles. We just accepted that this was Vince's time to die. Instead, we focused on enjoying our time together and making the most of each day. We also vowed to celebrate his life after his passing instead of mourning his loss.

Of course, this does not mean that we are not sad as we face our loss. James, Kate and I have all shed tears and have felt deep sorrow.

Death is a certainty for all us. We will all die at some point. It is our deep fear of death that keeps us in denial. We are afraid of the unknown, the uncertainty that accompanies death. We have no control over when and where our death will happen. Our anxiety and denial of death keep us from accepting the reality.

I want James and Kate to have a support system with them in case they need a break from the family dynamics during all the memorial events. I encourage them each to invite a best friend to fly with them to Philadelphia.

I ask my family to fly in for the funeral, as well. I am anxious about my own emotional well-being. Providing myself with a support system seems like a good idea. Since Vince's passing, my relationship with his family feels awkward, and I want to surround myself with people I can rely on to support me wholeheartedly. My mother and brother drop everything to join me for the weekend.

We make plans for my family, James and Kate and their friends to all converge at the Philadelphia airport on their way from California, Cincinnati and Chicago. Under the circumstances, coordinating everyone's travel is stressful, and by the time I reach the car rental kiosk, I'm exhausted and tense about the upcoming days. When the rental agent attempts to give me a Ford Explorer to accommodate eight adults—instead of the Yukon SUV I'd requested—I lose my composure. I release two months of strain and tension on the poor guy. He finds me a larger SUV. I circle the airport and pick up each group at its designated airline. Once I've collected everyone, we head to the hotel to check in.

We have about fifteen minutes to freshen up before we are expected at Vince's mother's house. She is hosting a casual Italian dinner for Vince's family and anyone who has flown in for the memorial service.

I'm calmed when we finally reach her house and we are in the presence of friends and family. James and Kate enjoy laughing and chatting with cousins and other relatives, and their friends who have come along fit right in. At one point, my sister-in-law takes me into the master bedroom to show me several photo collages she has put together for the memorial service. She spent many hours selecting the perfect images to represent each family member with Vince, including my mother. I am touched by all her effort and am overcome with emotion. I have been so busy preparing the children for the memorial service that I have forgotten I may experience some feelings of grief, too. I hug her tightly and thank her, deciding to leave the drama from weeks earlier in the past. I know she loved Vince and was disappointed she did not have a chance to see him one last time. Her anger with me was her way of dealing with his loss.

***

On Saturday morning, a traditional funeral limousine picks us up at our hotel. Everyone is dressed in black. James looks incredibly grown up in his dark pinstripe suit and tie. Kate has on a simple black sheath and pumps. There are seven of us in total: my mother, my brother, James and his best friend, Kate and her best friend and myself. The car takes us directly to the church.

When we arrive, we see Vince's family standing outside. The car pulls up behind another funeral limousine and parks in front of the church. The morning is chilly and there is a soft glow from the sun. Everyone greets each other, and Vince's family asks us to pose for photos. The children and I stand awkwardly in front of a small garden area.

"Are we supposed to smile?" Kate whispers.

I shrug my shoulders. Taking pictures at a funeral is a new experience for me. I don't think James and Kate are all that eager to capture the day this way. The finality of the service is weighing on them. I wish I had known about the photos, so I could have prepared them in the car for the situation. The three of us pose. Not knowing what else to do, I say, "Just smile."

More family and friends arrive. Vince's mother announces it is time to go into the church. The children and I slowly approach the door. None of us is eager to begin the morning.

Inside the church, my sister-in-law asks me where we are going to sit.

"Please, tell me where you would like us to sit," I say with a smile. I want to be respectful of Vince's mother and any plans she has set in place.

My sister-in-law returns a minute later and points across the aisle to the front two rows. "James and Kate can sit in the front row, and you and your family can sit in the second row."

I am confused. The front row is very small—just large enough for a few people. "Where will you be sitting?" I ask.

She points across the aisle to the center of the church. "Our family will sit there."

As I begin to ask why we are sitting separately from Vince's family, my mother-in-law walks up.

"We should line up," she whispers. Her eyes are dark pools filled with grief. Today will be incredibly difficult for her. She is burying her son. I cannot imagine her anguish.

"Where would you like the kids to stand?" I ask her.

She points to a spot and instructs me to stand there. James and Kate stand next to me, then Vince's brother, his wife, his son and lastly my mother-in-law. The church fills with friends, neighbors and family, and a line quickly begins to form with people wishing to express their condolences.

I am the first person in line to greet people. The majority of those entering the church are Vince's mother's friends, and they do not know who I am. Vince and I never lived in Philadelphia, so besides Vince's family members, no one knows my name. I feel pretty uncomfortable and hadn't expected to be in the line receiving condolences with the family in the first place. After all, I am Vince's ex-wife.

Initially, I introduce myself as Karen Scarpulla and shake hands, but people keep asking, "You are?"

So I begin to say, "Hello, I'm Karen Scarpulla, Vince's ex-wife."

This only leads to more confusion, odd looks and tilted heads.

So I change it up again. "Hello, I'm Karen Scarpulla, Vince's ex-wife, and these are our children James and Kate."

I am incredibly uncomfortable, but know I have to make the best of it. The quizzical looks and blank stares I receive make it evident that most of Vince's mother's friends are unaware that Vince and I have been divorced since 2006. My hope is to quickly move them down the line so they don't have time to ask questions.

Finally, my very dear friend, who is also Kate's godmother, arrives. I hug her and lose all composure. I am overwhelmed with sadness for my children and the stress of the receiving line. I am also surprised at the level of my own grief for Vince. We were married sixteen years, and he had been in my life for more than twenty-two years. I loved him very much during our marriage, especially as we started our family. Those were some of the best years with him. He is gone now, and I am startled by the overwhelming emptiness I am feeling.

We are instructed to take our seats. I point James and Kate to their pew, which only has room for three people. Their friends cannot sit with them, so I quickly move into their pew for comfort. Both James and Kate stare across the aisle at Vince's family.

Kate leans over to me. "Why are we sitting over here?"

"Nana told us sit here," I whisper.

"Aren't we part of the family anymore?" Suddenly the pipe organ bellows a mournful set of notes. Kate begins to cry softly, and I take her hand.

The ceremony is gloomy and sad. The music is ominous and depressing. I have been to other funerals where even though it is a sad occasion, the music is spiritually comforting. The ceremony focuses on loss, sadness and suffering. The kids and I sit in silence. One of Vince's cousins reads a passage from the Bible. He does a lovely job and kisses Vince's urn on the way to the lectern.

James will read the next passage. Many weeks earlier, Vince's mother had asked him if he would do a reading on the day of the memorial service. James is composed as he steps up to the lectern and proceeds to read with grace. It is a touching moment—Vince's son reading a passage from the Bible at his father's funeral. Tears fill the church, and I can feel Vince's presence.

Next is the Father's homily, which becomes more of a eulogy for Vince. The priest refers to Vince's family by pointing to the center front pew. He mentions each family member by name as he identifies Vince's mother, his brother, his sister-in-law and nephew. Kate turns to look at me. There is pain in her eyes and a tear rolls down her cheek. I can hardly believe what is happening. There is no mention of James and Kate. The Father continues with his homily, and as he looks down at his notes, I see a look of realization come across his face. He quickly adds that Vince has also left behind two lovely children, but does not mention their names or look at them. Kate glances at me again, and her anguish is visible on her face. While I know this was an oversight and not born out of malice, it has made James and Kate feel like outsiders at their own father's funeral, and the moment will be forever etched on their hearts.

James and Kate are teenagers who have lost their father too soon. Maybe people do not think they are suffering because the children have been focusing on moving forward with their lives. They have chosen to grieve in private and remain composed in public. Everyone grieves differently, and even though James and Kate do not openly show their grief, that does not mean they aren't in anguish.

We all have our own agendas and emotions at a service. The key during a memorial or funeral is to make sure those who are the closest to the loss are supported emotionally. Throughout the mass, James and Kate meet my eye with silent questions. In hindsight, I wish I had asked more questions about the service leading up to it, so that I could have set expectations for them. By preparing family members for the funeral and setting expectations, you remove any anxious anticipation and the possibility for hurt feelings.

We exit the church in silence. The finality of the next step hangs like a storm cloud over everyone's head. We head to our respective limousines and wait for what seems like hours to begin the procession.

The cemetery, where half of Vince's ashes will be laid to rest, is just down the road. A light drizzle adds to the gloomy mood. We sit in the car waiting until we see Vince's mother step out of her limousine. Then we walk in silence behind her to the gravesite, where other guests are standing nearby under a tent.

Vince will be buried in a family plot. Vince's paternal grandfather's and grandmother's graves are right next to Vince's father's. Vince's mother will be laid to rest next to Vince's father. The urn with Vince's ashes sits on a pedestal next to the grave. It will be buried on top of Vince's father's casket later after we leave the cemetery. The priest from church says a few words and a prayer, and then each family member steps forward to touch the urn and say goodbye one last time. I am overwhelmed with grief for my children. They are too young to lose their father. The finality of Vince's death engulfs each of us. James' grief is visible as he steps up and says goodbye. He can barely contain his tears as he swiftly heads to the waiting limousine. Kate walks up and says her goodbyes, and her sadness overwhelms her, as well. Her best friend is nearby to comfort her. We all stand there for a moment. One by one, we make our way to the car for the ride to the catering hall where Vince's mother will be hosting a lunch. The drive out of the cemetery is silent, but once we exit the cemetery gates, the car erupts in chatter. Everyone is relieved that the hardest part of the day is over. The lunch will be a celebration of Vince's life.

At the dining hall, we notice that the sign announcing our event has the family name misspelled. James is steamed and heads off to find a manager to rectify the situation. Emotions are raw. It has been a long morning for everyone. I head to the dining room to ask Vince's mother if there is anything I can do to help. I notice that there are two tables with "reserved" signs on them.

"Where would you like us to sit for lunch?" I ask.

"Your family can sit here." She points to a nearby reserved table.

We are stiff as we stand together for a moment. I have been struggling with my relationship with her over the last couple of months. She and I had always been incredibly close, even after the divorce. She used to tell her friends that I was the daughter she never had. Now there is a distance between us, and I am struggling to bridge the gap.

"It was a lovely service," I say.

"Yes." She smiles and turns her back to me to greet several of Vince's cousins.

I circle the room to greet guests and share stories with some of Vince's friends. James and Kate find me and ask where they should sit. I point to our table. They notice Vince's mother and a cousin sitting at a table nearby.

"We aren't sitting with Nana?" James asks.

"No. Nana said we should sit here," I say.

"So we are not sitting together as a family?"

"No." I say.

"Then can we sit somewhere else?" he asks.

"Sure. Sit wherever you like."

They choose a table across the room at the wall with some of their younger relatives. From my table, where I sit with my mother and brother, I periodically glance over at James and Kate. I'm relieved to see smiles on their faces after such a long, emotional morning.

Vince's family is consumed with sorrow, and Vince's mother is frozen in the moment. She is withdrawn and can barely speak to anyone. My family and I feel uncomfortable. We are not sure how to comfort her. I am feeling very awkward as the ex-wife. I realize that maybe my presence right now is a reminder of Vince's death since I was with him around the time he passed.

In this memorial setting, I do not fit into any of the traditional roles. I am James and Kate's mother, Vince's ex-wife, an ex-daughter-in-law and Vince's caregiver. I am aware that I am suffering from my own sense of loss, too. And my own anguish makes my interactions with Vince's mother and brother feel even clumsier.

Vince's friends begin to file in, and I make my way to the bar to greet them. They lighten the mood by sharing funny stories and memories of Vince. The crowd is smaller than anticipated. Vince expected that all his business acquaintances would fly in from all over the U.S., but instead it is a modest gathering of about sixty close friends and family. As lunch begins, we make our way to our respective tables.

Kate's godmother and godfather, very good friends of mine, stop at my table to say hello to my family. We invite them to join us. Several of Vince's business friends also end up joining us. Lunch is a quick affair. Vince's nephew says a blessing for the meal. The room fills with conversation and laughter as the individual tables share stories of Vince. I can feel Vince's spirit with us and know he would be pleased with the afternoon.

***

We all depart the following day for our homes, and James and his best friend fly back to school. Tears fill my eyes, and my voice catches in my throat as I bid James safe travels.

"Love you, buddy." I hug him.

He has grown into a young man right before my eyes. He and Kate have handled the weekend much better than I could have imagined. Today, James is excited to return to school and to move forward with his life.

Kate and I return home to Chicago and begin preparing for her college visit to Southern Methodist University in Dallas. Before Vince passed, he arranged for an old business associate, an SMU alumni, to set up a tour for Kate. Life must move forward.

***

The morning of our tour, the sun is shining bright, and the temperature is mild for Dallas. When we arrive, we are treated like VIPs. We tour the campus on a golf cart and then have meetings with the chairs in the public relations department, Kate's major. I am beaming as I watch her respond to interview questions. She's worked so hard over the past year, even through Vince's illness. She has a stellar GPA and has been handling the college application process all on her own. Our day on campus is long and overwhelming. There is so much information for Kate to absorb, and she looks exhausted as we depart campus.

The following day, we are invited to attend an SMU football game and tailgate party, known as "boulevarding." Our hosts pick us up at our hotel as rain begins to fall. We spend the next hour at their tent enjoying tailgate food and meeting other alumni. Everyone is excited to share his or her stories of being a student at SMU. Game time approaches, and the rain intensifies. Our seats are outside, so we opt to leave and head back to our hotel to dry off. Kate is worn out from yesterday's tour, and she wants to order room service and watch a movie. Later in the evening, we head to the Jacuzzi in the hotel to relax.

As we rehash the events of the last two days, the conversation turns to Vince. She is full of questions about him, our marriage and his life. I realize in this moment that she does not know much about her father. He never took the time to share stories of his life with her or James. During Vince's illness, he had asked me to arrange for someone to make a video. He thought this would be an excellent way to share his hopes, dreams and history with James and Kate. Each time I tried to schedule with the videographer, Vince would push it off. I suspect he was worried he would not be able to get through the video without breaking down in tears.

The first month that we all lived under one roof after Vince was diagnosed, we spent quite a bit of time together as a family. I joked that we had more family dinners in that first month then we had had in the last ten years of our marriage. But sadly, Vince began spending more and more of his time with friends and family in Philadelphia. I desperately wanted him to connect with James and Kate. I wanted him to have the opportunity to make up for all the lost time with them. The children felt he owed them time.

Kate and I continue to soak in the Jacuzzi, and she peppers me with questions. I know she is searching to make sense of his life and is looking for something "good" to hold onto.

"You know your dad was an excellent businessman and he always provided very well for us," I tell Kate. "He was incredibly dedicated to his career. This allowed him to provide your brother and you with opportunities he and I did not have growing up. The fact that SMU is a consideration for college is because your father worked so very hard."

"Why did you marry Dad?" she asks.

"I was young and fell in love with your father. He had a very commanding presence about him, and he was very goal oriented, just like I was. I thought we would be a great couple, and we were."

"Did you like being married?"

"Yes. I did. I liked being a wife and stay-at-home mom. I always felt blessed that your father took on the burden of being the sole breadwinner for the family. I tried to take care of everything else in his life. I always thought of us as a team." I pause for a second, but quickly continue. I know what her next question will be. "Divorcing your dad was one of the hardest decisions I have ever made. I wish things had been different, but when only one person is working on the relationship, it's not enough. Our bad marriage was beginning to affect you and James, and I felt I had to divorce him. Your father loves you and James more than he could ever tell you. Knowing he would not see you grow up after he passed was the hardest thing for him to accept."

"Why didn't he leave letters for us?" she asks.

"I think he just ran out of time."

I'm not sure why he never put the letters together. I pushed and prodded him everyday to write letters to James and Kate. I even offered to sit next to him with my laptop while he dictated what he wanted to say, but he refused. I assume it was too emotionally difficult for him.

Through our experience, I believe leaving behind a video or letters or both for your children is vital. It would be wonderful to hand James and Kate letters at various milestones like college graduation, the day each one gets married, or the birth of a child.

Since Vince's passing, I have learned of legacy letters. A legacy letter is a way to summarize your life history, values, beliefs, hopes and life lessons in one place. It outlasts you, extending your influence into the future. These letters can comfort and inspire those left behind forever.

Even though Vince had final conversations with James and Kate, these conversations were infused with emotion, and much of what was said and shared probably will be lost as the years go by. A legacy letter for James and Kate would have allowed Vince to be a positive part of each and every milestone. Letters are comforting. Surviving loved ones can refer back to them again and again. The words are concrete, and very little is left up to interpretation. Without a letter, James and Kate are left feeling empty and abandoned, unworthy of his time all over again. I will never forget the look of disappointment and hurt when Kate learned Vince did not leave her a letter. I encourage people to take time now to write a legacy letter to their children and family members even if you are not dying or sick. These letters will provide counsel and comfort for years to come.

I have recently learned of a wonderful organization, the Association of Personal Historians (APH). It is a great resource for locating people in your area to help you capture your personal history. With technology there are so many unique ways to capture one's legacy either through memoirs or biographies, photo narratives, video, genealogy research and legacy letters.

"I miss him," Kate says.

"I know you do, and he is so incredibly proud of you," I say.

We have been in the Jacuzzi for several hours. Our hands and feet look like raisins. We have reminisced about family experiences, vacations, birthday parties and finally Vince's passing. Neither of us wants to leave the warmth of the water, but it is late. We head back to the room relaxed and sleepy. I can see Kate moving through the grief process. She forgave Vince before he passed, and tonight she looks for memories of loving times with her father rather than focusing on her current pain. This is another step toward her healing. She is handling her grief so well, and she amazes me.

***

Back home, Kate and I are ready to begin painting the interior of Vince's house. Kate has moved from the basement bedroom to a bedroom upstairs, which is just down the hall from mine. Kate and I will live here until she goes off to college, and I will remain at the house until the kids get settled in their new lives after college. Vince had wanted to paint the house and refinish the hardwood floors when I moved in, but I encouraged him to let me handle it later. The thought of having workmen in the house while he was going through chemotherapy and radiation was not appealing. Vince had very little patience and did not like change.

Now it is time to begin the renovation process. Vince had set aside money in the trust for household renovations and repairs. Fresh paint will allow us to have a fresh start, create closure and create a homey environment. The kids will have an opportunity to design their own rooms. Vince never put any effort or money into making James' and Kate's rooms feel like *their* rooms. A teenager's room is his or her sanctuary, an escape, a nest. I am determined that they both have a room that they will enjoy coming home to as they return from college each year. The renovation will be a long process and take more than six weeks.

The month of October flies by for Kate and me. We have three college visits in the Los Angeles area. I am happy to have a busy month and am relieved that Kate is focused on college. Staying busy allows her to move forward with her life and begin letting go of her grief in little pieces. While in L.A., we drive by our old house in Redondo Beach where James was born. We visit Malibu, West L.A. and Santa Monica. Our days are spent touring colleges, and in the evenings, we enjoy some retail therapy and delicious dinners. We even squeeze in an afternoon by the pool.

During our trip, Kate recalls her very first visit to Los Angeles with Vince. She fondly remembers walking on Santa Monica pier, eating lunch on the veranda at the Loews Hotel, tasting caviar for the first time, driving around with the top down and keeping an eye out for celebrities. I think that trip may have been her favorite memory of Vince.

***

James is entrenched in his first year at the University of Cincinnati. He keeps himself busy with school. On occasion, he has called to talk about his grief or to share how much he misses talking to Vince about sports.

While growing up, neither child ever had daily interaction with Vince because of his travel schedule. When he was home on the weekends, he rarely spent time with the kids. Now, it is not his daily absence that is causing their sorrow. Their suffering and grief come from knowing their father is gone. They are also fearful because they have been left with just one parent. What if something happens to me? Who will be left to care for them? These fears weigh on both James and Kate. It will take many months for their anxiousness to subside. All I can do is reassure them that I plan to be around a long time, nagging and loving them. The reality is that no one knows when we will die, but I do everything I can now to put them at ease.

***

During the month of October, Kate has felt Vince's spirit on many occasions. One morning she tells me that she woke up in the middle of the night and saw a fuzzy male figure floating in the corner of her room. The figure had dark hair and was wearing an orange T-shirt, just like the one Vince had on when he passed.

On another morning, she comes up to my room and asks me if I was in her room.

She'd heard someone calling her name last night. The voice sounded just like Vince's. Kate said she then used the bathroom, and upon returning to bed, she stepped on the corner of a very large fashion book she had received as a Christmas gift. The corner of the book hurt her foot. In the morning she woke up to find the book in bed next to her.

"I think he was in my room," she says.

"Why do you say that?" I ask.

"Did you put the book in my bed?"

"No. I didn't go into your room last night." We both knew that Vince must have put the book in bed so she wouldn't hurt her foot again.

***

As the month comes to an end, it is Kate's birthday. This is her first birthday without Vince. This will be the first of many "firsts." Vince had wanted to live long enough to spend one last birthday with Kate, but the universe was working on a different timetable.

It is just after midnight when Kate comes running into my room and leaps into bed.

"What's wrong?" I ask.

I am half asleep as she begins to talk.

"I saw someone standing in my room. There is a man with dark hair standing in front of my window. It looks like he's holding something. I think it's a birthday cake."

"Who do you think it is?" I ask.

"I think it's Dad," she whispers.

"Me too. It's past midnight, which means it is officially your birthday. I'm sure he wanted to be the first one to wish you happy birthday. He loves you so much, and I know how much he wanted to live long enough to have one more birthday with you."

She smiles and her lips begin to quiver. She misses him so much, and his visit is comforting for her. I hug her tightly and we both begin to cry.

CHAPTER THREE

NOVEMBER — NEW BEGINNINGS

*"Grief is in two parts. The first is loss.
The second is the remaking of life."*
— Anne Roiphe

The process of refinishing hardwood floors, ordering new appliances and painting every room in the house is stressful. Workmen are present in our house every day, Monday through Saturday. At one point, Kate and I live in one room, the master suite, to avoid the maze of painting scaffolds, papered floors and tarps. Kate is stressed and wants the house to be finished. I thought it would be easier to do everything all at once—just like ripping off a Band-Aid.

It has been just two months since Vince's passing. I have to drive to Cincinnati for a conference and will have an opportunity to visit James. I am so excited to see him. I scurry around preparing for my trip and make sure Kate has a place to stay while I'm away.

It's a sunny fall day in Chicago, one of my favorite times of year. Murphy and I stroll to the mailbox, and I am filled with love and gratitude. The children are moving forward with their lives and allowing their pain to pass. Renovations are underway, and I am working to rebuild my business. Life is good.

Murphy and I head back to the house with my bundle of mail. I sort through the stack and notice a large manila envelope with an attorney's return address. I know immediately this is the lease agreement from Vince's estate. I set it aside with the knowledge that signing the lease is just a formality. I will deal with it later.

Vince promised the children and me that we could remain in his home as long as we wanted. The only requirement is that I must pay all the utilities and homeowner's association dues every month. The agreement is a gift that will provide me with breathing room so I don't have to stress about finances while I support the children as they finish school. Vince's home had become our family home during the ten months that we lived together. As the children return from school, they will have family memories to come home to. I am comforted knowing he loved us enough at the end to make the children's college years easier for us.

Later in the day, I take a break from the current marketing projects I am working on to read through the lease. I begin to read the first page, and my stomach turns upside down. I feel like I am going to be sick. My eyes fill with tears.

I can hardly believe what I am reading. I continue reviewing the lease. Vince has instructed the trust that I may live in the home for the next two years. In addition, I will be required to pay rent to the trust each month. At the end of two years, the trust will sell the home, and we will need to move. I am devastated. Emotionally crushed.

Surely it must be a mistake.

But part of me knows it is not a mistake. I feel like such a fool and an idiot.

Did my gift of caring for him and reuniting him with his children mean nothing to him? Did he not understand the sacrifice I made, giving up my life for the last ten months?

I gave him everything I had, emotionally and physically. It is almost too horrible to believe. The irony is that I will pay James and Kate's trust rent to live in their house and take care of them.

I feel the anger well up inside of me. I was in such a good place with Vince when he passed away. That last night together I knew I had forgiven him. I had nothing but love and compassion in my heart for him. He was James and Kate's father, and most of all, a human being who was dying far too young. I had worked hard to forgive all the horrible things he had done as a husband and father. Now, as I look at the lease agreement, I feel victimized and abandoned all over again.

Since moving in with Vince to care for him, I had been living off of the proceeds of my previous home. Vince had stopped paying child support, which had created a financial strain on me. When I first offered to move in, Vince had agreed to assume all the household expenses and said he would take care of everything. This did not happen. The expenses associated with raising two teenagers quickly added up with gas money, groceries, car repairs and cell phone bills. I covered most of it. I also paid for storage rental every month to store my personal belongings because they would not fit in Vince's home. Plus, as my caregiver role grew more time consuming, I spent less time focusing on work. My absence began impacting the company's revenue.

I decide to call the trustee. Surely there has been some lapse with paperwork, an omission or oversight on the attorney's part.

I preface our conversation with, "I am really sorry. I am going to try to talk to you without losing my composure, but I am really upset."

"What's wrong?" he asks.

"This lease agreement is not what Vince told me it would be. He told us that we could stay in this house as long as we wanted, so the kids would have a family home to return to," I explain. "I don't understand. This is nothing like he and I discussed." My eyes begin to fill with tears.

"Don't worry about this," he says. "I will call the attorney. Maybe they didn't have time before Vince passed to change things. Don't worry. We will work this out."

His words give me comfort, but in the back of my mind I know that Vince lied.

I'd already received a shock regarding the insurance money. Per our divorce decree, Vince and I were both required to carry a certain amount of life insurance until the last child turned eighteen. In the event of one parent's death, this would provide money to the parent left behind to finish raising the children. Shortly after Vince died, I contacted our insurance broker. As we began discussing the details of the insurance policy, he told me that I would receive a check in the mail for a specified amount— half of what I thought it would be.

"That amount is not accurate. It should be double that," I said.

"Well, let me check," said the broker. I heard him tapping away at his computer. "No. I show that Vince lowered the value on the insurance policy six months ago."

This was an absolute blow to me. Vince had always reminded me through the last ten months, not worry about my finances and business because I was still the beneficiary on his life insurance. Knowing he had purposefully lowered his insurance policy makes me sick to my stomach. I ask the broker how much money Vince saved on the premium. His answer shocks me.

"$468.00."

What an unconscionable act.

Why did he lower the insurance policy? Why did he mandate that the children and I must move out in two years?

I thought he and I were in a good place before he passed. I had forgiven him for all the years of hurt.

Did he still harbor ill feelings toward me?

His actions make me feel as if he still held a grudge against me for divorcing him.

Could this even be possible in light of how lovingly I cared for him until the end?

It is more than I can bear to think about.

***

My business partner and I make the five-hour drive to Cincinnati. I am hoping to have dinner with James, but he has a paper due and is studying for midterms. I drop off several bags of groceries at his apartment and hug him briefly. He suggests we have lunch the next day.

I toss and turn all night long, feeling sick to my stomach. I wonder why Vince went back on his word. I replay in my mind a day a few weeks before he passed when I was unraveling. I was having a particularly hard time. Vince called me into his bedroom where he and his mom were chatting. He asked what was wrong. I explained I had a large RFP (Request For Proposal) due for a potential client, a major corporation. I was struggling to juggle taking care of Vince, our home and the children.

"What is the value of the contract? I will write you a check," he offered.

"It's $250,000 over three years. It's a really big contract," I said on the verge of tears. Exhaustion was beginning to settle in.

"I'll give you $25,000 so you don't have to worry about responding," he said.

That is ten percent of the value of the RFP,

obviously not enough to cover the loss of the business if I do not respond, but I also knew that his offer was an empty one. He often made bold gestures but rarely followed through. I declined his absurd offer. He asked what else he could do to help.

"There's nothing you can do right now," I told him. "Please, just tell me you took care of the house?" At that point Vince's care was consuming all of my time, and I was unable to work on any marketing projects. I could barely keep up with emails and phone calls from current clients.

"Yes, I did," he said. "You and the kids can stay as long as you want with no worries."

"You called the attorney? You took care of the house?"

"Yes. I took care of it." He looked me straight in the eye and assured me.

Now, looking back on this moment, I wish I would have accepted the $25,000 check, but I know deep in my heart it never would have materialized. Besides, it was a drop in the bucket compared to all the potential lost revenue, not to mention lost child support.

The tears stream down my cheeks. I am heart broken.

How could he lie to my face as he lay in bed dying?

I am exasperated that I am now confronted with the demons from our past. All the old hurts and broken promises come flooding back to me. I worked so hard to forgive him before he died to release me from our past, but now the past reminds me of how awful he could be. I feel a new grudge taking hold in my heart and exhaustion settles in as I drift off to sleep.

***

The following afternoon, my business partner and I pick up James in front of his apartment. He directs us to downtown Cincinnati where we have lunch at Tom and Chee, a famous grilled cheese and tomato soup restaurant. He looks great, and we chat about school and how it feels to be winding down his first semester. He is enjoying college and Cincinnati. We spend a couple of hours with him and then drop him back at school. I will see him the following week for Thanksgiving. I am so proud of him and how well he is handling Vince's passing, school and how he is maturing into a young man full of life.

"I've never seen James smile so much," says my business partner.

I am overcome with emotion and pride. We head to the interstate ready for the drive back to Chicago. I try to put thoughts of Vince and the house out of my mind as we chat, but my buzzing cell phone interrupts our conversation.

It's the trustee of Vince's estate. He explains that with any trust, the letter of the trust must be followed. He had hoped that Vince's attorney would have been aware of the agreement between Vince and me. However, Vince had never contacted the attorney regarding the new terms. A lump forms in my throat and tears fill my eyes.

I will have to pay monthly rent to live in the house with the children for two years. I feel like I have been sucker punched in the stomach. My heart is broken. Instead of giving me the breathing room he promised, I feel as if Vince has taken away my oxygen tank. I am now under a two-year time constraint. The house will be sold as James begins his third year and Kate begins her second year of college. I am hurt that our family meant so very little to Vince as he died.

"I understand," is all I can choke out before I hang up.

***

I return home and decide that I must share the news with the children. As Kate and I enjoy dinner together that evening, I broach the subject.

"I have some news. I spoke with the trustee, and it turns out that your father's trust mandates that we can only stay in the house for two years, and only if I pay rent to the trust. The house has to be sold in November of 2014."

She has a puzzled look on her face. "But Dad promised we could stay in the house while we are in college. Can the trust make us move?"

"Yes. The trust is your dad's final wish, and he never told his attorney to change anything with regards to the house."

"Can we go to court and fight it? James and I can tell them what Dad told us."

"Don't worry. I will work it out."

The reality is there is no working it out. Vince has made his wishes very clear. James and Kate both offer to speak with the trustee and go to court if needed to seek help. I'm uncomfortable dragging them into court. My purpose in moving in together was to provide the children with some new happy memories of their father. Fighting the trust and engaging in a court battle will dredge up old hurts and wounds for them. I don't want to make the situation any more dramatic than it already is. I choose to accept Vince's wishes for the sake of the children. In two years, we will need to find another place to live.

***

The Thanksgiving holiday arrives. It is such a comforting feeling to have both children under one roof. We are blessed to have wonderful friends in Chicago who have become a sort of extended family for us. Friends invite us over for Thanksgiving dinner, and we are grateful to not have to celebrate our first holiday without Vince in his home.

I head over to our friends' house mid day to help prepare the meal. Our hosts are gourmet cooks, and I am passionate about food and love cooking, as well. I spend the afternoon chopping, stirring and enjoying champagne and great wine. The children arrive later in the afternoon—just in time for appetizers. Dinner is amazing with roasted turkey and all the traditional side dishes with just a bit of gourmet flair.

We spend time reminiscing about Vince and sharing funny stories. There is lots of laughter, the perfect medicine for everyone's grief. Vince's family and his best friend call during dinner to wish James and Kate a happy Thanksgiving. The children leave after dessert, and I stay for a while longer enjoying the good company. As I drive home, I know that going to court to fight the trust is not an option. The kids hold tightly to their good memories of Vince. I can't bear the thought of tarnishing their memories or creating a rift in their relationship with him. Even though he is dead, they both need to have positive thoughts of their father. A court battle will just remind everyone of Vince's broken promises and dredge up old hurts and wounds. I moved in with Vince so the children could salvage their relationship with him or create a new one. Taking this battle to court will potentially destroy all the good that has been gained. I just can't do that. Everything happens for a reason. I have to believe that there will be a silver lining for us down the road.

The two-year time constraint will change the landscape of the next two years for me. I will not have money to help James and Kate with college expenses as I struggle to rebuild my company. They will need to be completely independent, living on the college money Vince left behind. I will be under constant pressure, knowing in two years we will have to move. I can purchase Vince's home from the trust at the end of two years, but this will not be financially possible. My life will be in limbo. Vince's home is the last home where we lived together as a family—reunited for just ten short months. I know no matter where I move after this, it will never feel like home to James and Kate.

I am crushed. My heart aches with the pain of Vince's betrayal. The thought that he lied to my face on his deathbed is unbelievable. But there are no excuses. Vince was lucid until forty-eight hours before he passed. He had many opportunities to follow through on his commitment to the children and me. But I realize I cannot control what has happened. His actions are in the past. I can only control my response to them moving forward. I have worked hard to forgive the past. Tonight I decide to forgive yet again and to release myself from the pain I am feeling.

I realize he must have still been so angry with me about the divorce. I feel sad for him that he preferred to hate me rather than accept the love and compassion I showed him. I cared for him with love, tenderness and patience. I endured many sleepless nights at the end to make sure he was comfortable and safe. Most importantly, I reunited him with his children, even though it was something he had not earned. He died in his home, just as he wanted.

His choices are his own, and his grudge against me was greater than his appreciation for my help or even his family. I forgive him not because I am condoning his actions, but because I love myself. I will not allow Vince to plant hatred and bitterness in my heart any longer. I release myself from putting any energy towards his actions. He no longer has the power to hurt me. I choose to forgive him for his behavior so I can be happy. I am comforted knowing that I did the right thing by caring for him. My children are adjusting so well because they had time together with their father. I move on filled with forgiveness, because I deserve to be happy.

CHAPTER FOUR

DECEMBER — CHRISTMAS LOST

"Maybe Christmas doesn't come from a store, maybe Christmas perhaps means a little bit more."
— the Grinch

When the children were smaller, Christmas was all about Santa Claus and the sea of toys under the tree Christmas morning. We set out a glass of milk and homemade cookies for Santa and carrots for the reindeer. As the children grew older, I tried to shift their focus from gifts under the tree to the "true" meaning of the holiday: giving. We would spend time shopping for presents for families less fortunate. I would take the children to Target, and we would stuff backpacks full of goodies to give away. The kids always enjoyed these shopping excursions.

As they continued to grow older, we would read *Chicken Soup for the Soul* Christmas stories about the magical gifts of the holiday, which center on the true meaning of the season. Each year, I would look for opportunities to create new family traditions.

After the divorce, Vince and I traded the days each year in which we spent the holidays with the kids. One year, I'd celebrate with James and Kate on Christmas Eve and the next year on Christmas Day.

The previous holiday before Vince's passing, we had all flown to Philadelphia to be with Vince and his family. Even though we were hopeful that his chemo and radiation would buy him time, deep down, he and I knew it would be his last Christmas. Christmas of 2011 was not about the material gifts that we bought each other; it was about spending time together as a family.

Now that Vince is gone, I hope to create some new traditions with James and Kate. As the holidays approach, the children remind me that it was Vince's wish that they always spend Christmas with Vince's family. Even though I want the kids to remain connected to Vince's family, I have to admit that I'm a little frustrated. I want to be with my kids.

Vince's ego was so large, that even on his deathbed, he never considered my wishes for the holidays or my family. During our marriage, I allowed Vince to alienate me from my family. The very last holiday I had spent with my family was Thanksgiving 1992 when we lived in Los Angeles before James was born. The children never spent a holiday with my family during our marriage. After the divorce, I was able to take the children to California for Thanksgiving on a couple of occasions when it was my year to have them for that holiday. However, we could never spend Christmas with my family, because Vince and I switched off Christmas Day and Christmas Eve each year. This made it impossible to take them to California for any length of time. I am frustrated, that even now from beyond the grave, he continues to control our holiday. Looking back, I wish I had insisted that the children spend more Christmases with me.

James and Kate are adamant that they honor Vince's wish that they spend the holidays with his family. I am hurt that the children are not considering spending Christmas with me. I have spent so many Christmases alone since the divorce. With Vince gone, I was looking forward to spending the entire Christmas holiday with my children.

I am surprised to find out that Vince's brother and his wife are spending the holidays with her daughter and grandchildren.

"Nana will be alone," James tells me. "Kate and I have to go to Philadelphia."

The reality is that Vince's mother's family surrounds her. Her sister and her husband, their three sons and numerous nieces and nephews and other family members all live within a twenty-mile radius. She will have dinner at her sister's home just like every holiday.

Vince's mother has graciously extended a holiday invitation to me, but I am no longer a part of Vince's family. Since the children will be going to Philadelphia, I have decided to spend Christmas with my own family in California, especially since this will be my father's last Christmas. He has been given six months to live.

Early the next morning, the kids and I gather in the living room waiting for our car to the airport. We are all scheduled to leave on the same day for our respective Christmases. James is not feeling well. Several days ago he slipped on the ice and is still suffering the effects of a mild concussion. He is feeling nauseated, has a headache and does not want to fly. He encourages Kate to continue on to Philadelphia without him.

"Nana will be sad if you don't go. It is her first Christmas without Dad," he says.

I offer to stay behind with James, but he insists I fly to California to be with my father. I am uncomfortable leaving James at home, but he is an adult, and we have neighbors next door if he needs help. I am so torn between being a supportive and responsible mother and being a good daughter. If only I could cut myself in half and be in two places at once. I decide to fly to California. I will only be gone three days. I am sad. This is not how I envisioned Christmas.

***

Kate arrives in Philadelphia to find that the cousins who are her age are traveling and will not be attending the festivities. Kate is disappointed she will be spending the holidays with all of Vince's adult aunts, uncles and cousins. A crowd of older men, mainly Vince's cousins—who are all too busy watching sports to even notice her—gathers in the living room. Of Vince's three cousins, only one is still married, and his wife has her hands full watching her three-year old grandson. Throughout the evening, I receive a multitude of text messages from Kate expressing that she'd rather be in California. I am frustrated with myself for not speaking up to Vince's mother and insisting the kids spend Christmas with my family and me for once. At one point, I offer to put Kate on a plane so she can be with me, but she decides to stay.

She tells me that at Christmas dinner a toast is made in honor of Vince, and everyone acknowledges Vince's mother's loss. The conversation centers around how this must be a difficult holiday for her without her son.

I receive another text from Kate: "I guess they forget that he was my dad."

It is easy to overlook people when they are not grieving outwardly. Vince's mother is mired in her grief and talks often of her loss. Kate mourns privately. Her grief is not visible. Grief comes in all forms, and even though someone is not outwardly mourning, acknowledging his or her loss is still important.

Kate expresses her disappointment to me over the phone.

"Why am I the only one who honored Dad's wish that we always spend the holidays together? Dad's own brother didn't even stay home to be with his mother. This is the worst Christmas."

"Maybe they don't feel as strongly as you do about respecting your dad's wishes," I say.

"I'm not going next year," she says.

"I understand. I don't blame you. Frankly, next year I am going to insist that you and James spend the holidays with me. I have given up many holidays for your dad and his family. Next year we will be together."

I realize that James and Kate took Vince's last words very seriously. They honor his wishes as a way of connecting themselves to him. Vince's brother has his own family and set of priorities and that may not include Vince's mandate.

"I think it is great that you try to honor your father's wishes, but this is your life to lead now and you should choose what feels best for you," I say.

"I'm the only one who did what Dad asked."

"I know. Next year will be different."

***

On the plane home from California, I replay the events of this holiday season over again in my mind. I am angry with myself for not loving myself enough to ask for what I wanted, Christmas with my children. In this moment, it is not about forgiving Vince but rather about forgiving myself. Sometimes we need to forgive ourselves for the choices we have made in order to release the pain.

I've learned so much in the past year about forgiveness. Not many people can find forgiveness with an ex-spouse. I am grateful that I created a process that has worked for me. I gaze out the window of the airplane and think back over all the various reactions I have had from people when I tell my story. Many say they could never move back in with their ex, especially to take care of him or her.

I recall the day that Vince and I sat in the living room laughing about the fact that a TLC producer had interest in doing a show about our story.

I can hear Vince's voice: "You should write a book about us," he had said.

The seed was planted back then. Now, on the flight home, I realize I have been given the gift of forgiveness and I must share it with everyone. After all, if I can forgive Vince, certainly I can inspire anyone to forgive. A smile spreads across my face as I think about the possibility of writing a book.

***

Once we are all back in Chicago, the kids and I spend time together sharing stories and family gossip from our holidays. We all agree that next Christmas will be different. We will spend the holidays together in Chicago creating new traditions. I am overjoyed. No more lonely Christmases.

CHAPTER FIVE

JANUARY — MILESTONES

"Life isn't a matter of milestones but of moments."
— Rose Kennedy

The new year begins with a hush. I am acutely aware that this will be a year of many, many moments— some of them large and some of them so small, they may not be noticed. Life is moving on for us as a family. James returns to college this week to begin his second semester, and Kate will graduate early from high school in just a few weeks.

I am having a tough time finding my groove with work. I used to love working long hours and thought nothing of working through the weekends. But now—after watching Vince die and knowing how hard he worked and how much he sacrificed in the name of materialism—I don't have the same zeal for my business and all the long hours required to run a marketing company. My passion for marketing is gone. Watching someone die puts life in perspective, and I realize that it is just as important to enjoy life as it is to build a career.

I have officially committed myself to the goal of writing a book. I want to share my experiences learning to forgive and also what it is like to have a loved one die at home. I'm just not sure how to get started. Part of the problem is my exhaustion. I feel as if I could sleep for hours like a bear curling up for his winter's nap. I feel listless, and I am aware that my emotions are flat. It has been just three months since Vince passed. Over those three months I have been so focused on the funeral, James and Kate and renovating the house, that I have not taken time to regroup emotionally or to process my own grief.

I recognize that I am struggling with many emotions that I have not taken time to acknowledge: anger, sadness, a sense of failure, abandonment and victimization. I lie in bed checking my email on my phone and come across a message from Wayne Dyer's website. There is still space available at his two-day workshop in Maui. I have always been a fan of Wayne Dyer. My brother introduced me to his work with the movie, *The Shift*. I highly recommend it if you have not watched it yet. At this point in my life, I have read many of his books, and I follow his daily quotes of inspiration. Many months earlier, before Vince passed, I received an email with upcoming Wayne Dyer events. As I reviewed the list, I noticed that he would be hosting this event in Hawaii, where he would speak about finding "love." Of course, the idea is to find love in oneself. At the time, I had tucked the thought of Maui in the back of my head as something I could possibly treat myself to in the future. Now, as I see that there is still space open in the workshop, it hits me that I need to go to reenergize myself.

Kate wanders into my room and climbs into bed with me. I suddenly have a vision of Kate and me in Maui having some quality mother-daughter time together.

"When is your last day of finals?" I ask.

I can't believe our good fortune. Her last day is the day before we would need to leave for Maui.

Kate had decided her sophomore year that she wanted to graduate early from high school. She is an old soul, and the majority of her friends have always been older. Once senior year arrived, she was ready to move on. She always took the maximum amount of classes so she could finish in January. It is funny how things have a way of working themselves out. She will now have the opportunity to have some downtime, rest and relaxation before college starts.

"I am going to attend a Wayne Dyer workshop in Maui in a few days. How would you feel about going with me?" I ask.

I explain to her that the workshop is during the weekend and that after the conference we could enjoy Maui together. She is excited at the mention of escaping the Chicago winter. While I had visions of traveling on my own, I know it is important to make sure James and Kate don't feel abandoned by me in any way. Plus, it will be so much fun to have some mother-daughter time.

I am concerned about the costs, but I look at this conference as an investment in my future. I am sure it will help me jumpstart my writing. I also know I am having trouble processing my grief.

My friends and family are having trouble being supportive, because they cannot fathom my personal sadness over Vince's death. He had created so much chaos in my life for so many years that they think I should be grateful he is gone so that he can no longer hurt me. I see their point, but am still consumed with sadness. I feel sad, confused and heartbroken. But most of all, I feel like a failure. While I take comfort and satisfaction in the fact that I reunited Vince with his children, I am sad that I never was able to influence him to open his heart. I am disappointed he never let his guard down. I could not convince him to leave his fear behind and embrace the love that was all around him.

I also have my own grief over Vince's loss. He is the father of the two most important people in my life, and I did love him once. I cling to the hope that writing the book will be a cathartic experience for me. Maybe I will find relief for my grief during the process.

I drag my laptop into bed, and Kate and I begin making arrangements. Planning a vacation with Kate helps to lift my blue feelings for the afternoon.

***

The next morning, I am still battling exhaustion and sorrow. I am always in search of tools, books or anything that will help me live a more fulfilling, healthy and centered life. Many of my friends have used Reiki as a way to keep their chakras aligned, and I am curious.

There are seven major chakras in our body. They are circles of spiritual power that balance, store and distribute our life energy. When our chakras are out of alignment, this can affect our physical, mental and spiritual health. Reiki is a healing technique in which a therapist can channel energy into the patient by means of touch. This energy activates the natural healing processes of the patient's body to restore physical and emotional well-being. Reiki massage balances the life force energy of the seven chakras. By placing his or her hands on or above the corresponding area, the therapist can read the energy for each chakra and can see where there are blocks to the energy force.

A friend refers me to a Reiki therapist who has helped her align her chakras. I am desperate to meet with the therapist before my trip to see Wayne Dyer. I want to make sure my body and energy are in complete alignment so that I can maximize the experience of the seminar.

I arrive at the therapist's house with an open mind. She practices Reiki in her home in a suburb not far from where I live. As with anything new I try, I approach our encounter with an open mind and spirit. I am eager for any help she can provide. We begin our session by meditating for a few minutes just to relax my breathing and body. I settle into a small chair in the room with my feet firmly planted on the ground, sitting tall and hands folded in my lap. I find it very difficult to meditate and still my mind, but I try to focus on my breathing and clear my head of any thoughts that pop into my consciousness.

I am dressed comfortably in leggings, socks and a large oversized sweater. It is winter in Chicago and very cold. After meditating, I climb up on the massage table, and the therapist covers me with a large blanket. She uses a small blue crystal on a string to expose the chakras that are not in alignment. She begins at the top of my head and works down to my feet. She carefully holds the crystal above each chakra. If the chakra in question is functioning and open, the crystal will rotate in a circle. The stronger the energy, the faster the crystal will rotate. If a person's energy is blocked, the crystal will barely move or not move at all.

The seventh chakra, the crown chakra, is at the top of the head. My crown chakra is completely out of balance. The crystal barely moves. When this chakra is out of balance, a person may have trouble with self-confidence, fear and anxiety. The therapist continues working down my body to check each chakra. My fifth chakra, the throat chakra, is also out of alignment. Situated at the base of the neck, it influences communication and creativity. Over the past year, I have often experienced sore throats and have actually lost my voice. This is a clear sign that this chakra is not functioning properly.

As she approaches my fourth chakra, the heart chakra, the crystal pendulum swings in a circular motion, indicating this chakra is not blocked. I breathe a sigh of relief. When the heart chakra is in balance, a person can feel unconditional love. The heart chakra allows us to help others. Rejuvenation, rebirth, success, growth, prosperity and development all work together so we can influence and support people in our life.

She continues down my body with the pendulum crystal. My third chakra, located in the solar plexus, controls personal power. As the pendulum remains still, she explains that when this chakra is unbalanced it can lead to feelings of frustration. I am aware that I am feeling overwhelmed and lost. I feel as if I am drowning and every so often my head springs to the surface for a breath. I have been trying to rebuild my company after my absence caring for Vince.

A year earlier, my business partner and I had realigned our responsibilities within our marketing company. My responsibility is to drive all marketing related business and to execute all marketing projects for our clients. Back then, I also expanded our offerings to include workshops for small business owners. This had required a financial commitment from my personal bank account to cover the initial costs of launching this program. My partner's role is to provide sales representation for several companies. This keeps her on the road, and, unfortunately with the types of two-to-three-year sales cycle contracts we sign, it takes a while before we generate revenue. The marketing side of our company has always supported the business side, and it covers the overhead each month. As I cared for Vince, I barely had time to execute the few projects we had in the pipeline. There was certainly no time to chase new business. Now that I am back to work full time, I am feeling the financial pressure to rebuild quickly, and I feel powerless.

The Reiki therapist sets to work beginning to look for the break in the circle of energy that is causing unbalance. Something in my past may have created a break. Until these past traumas or experiences are cleared, a chakra will remain out of balance. She discovers one of my chakras is blocked because of a childhood car accident with my parents. Apparently, I have unresolved communication around the accident. I am completely unaware that I was angry with my parents for causing the accident. I had never fully expressed my anger, which I had buried since I was twelve years old. Unresolved communication has always been a common theme in my life, a behavior I adopted at an early age.

Over the next thirty minutes, she focuses on realigning my chakras. Once she is done, she rechecks each chakra with the pendulum. This time the pendulum swings in a wide circular motion over each chakra, demonstrating that all of my energy is open. A tingling sensation courses through my entire body as my spirit connects with the universal power surrounding me. My body and mind feel light and energized. I am relaxed and content. She then tells me that she can sometimes read other people's energy that surrounds a person. She was quick to explain that she is not clairvoyant. She simply possesses the ability to feel other people's energy that may be swirling.

"Would you like me to read the energy around

you?" she asks.

"Yes," I say, not knowing what to expect.

She is quiet for a while and then she slowly begins to speak.

I am shocked at what she has to say. She knows nothing about me. She only knows my name, not anything regarding the events of the previous year or my life.

"There is a tall man with dark hair who wants to thank you for taking care of him," she says. "He says he can never repay you for what you did. You showed him great kindness, and he is grateful."

She asks if I know who this man is. My eyes are closed but tears stream down my cheeks as I mumble, "yes."

"Do you want me to continue," she asks.

"Yes."

"He wants you to know that he is sorry that he was such a bad husband.

"I apologize for the words I am going to use. I am just saying what he is saying," she explains.

"I was an asshole," she says.

With this sentence I am sure it is Vince speaking to me.

"I have been shown several portals and have seen how my life could have been so different. I had the opportunity to have a different life, but I chose different paths."

He talks about Murphy our dog, who showed him unconditional love and how he learned what it means. Any remaining doubt that it is Vince dissipates.

"Most of all, I am sorry about the money. I shouldn't have given you less. I shouldn't have changed the insurance. You gave me my family back, and that was worth more than I could ever give you."

"Does this make sense to you?" the therapist asks.

I nod my head yes. The lump in my throat makes speaking impossible.

Vince continues, "I know you are very worried about money and your future, but you don't have to be. I have seen your future, and your road is paved with gold. You will be very successful. You just need to write the book. You will receive lots of accolades. Your future is bright and paved with gold," he reiterates.

A warm glow washes over me, and I tingle with energy once again as the therapist brings our session to a close. I slowly sit up and perch on the edge of the table for a moment.

"Are you okay?" the therapist asks.

"Yes. I am actually relieved to know he feels sorry for what he did."

"I could see he was very sorry," she says. "He hung his head and was full of shame and remorse as he spoke to me."

I pay her and thank her for the session. As I drive home, I replay the entire scene once again, not wanting to forget a single element of this event. Vince was apologetic. I have never experienced that side of Vince. In fact, I don't think Vince has ever apologized for anything he has ever done to hurt me.

I wonder if in death he found forgiveness for me. Did he finally forgive me for divorcing him? Most of all, I hope he finds forgiveness for himself. He made a lot of mistakes and hurt a lot of people, but he conducted his life the best way he knew how. I hope he forgives himself for his choices and knows that I have forgiven him, as well.

***

Several days later, Kate and I fly to Dallas from Chicago and then board a seven-hour flight to Maui. We are excited to have some time away together, and I am even more excited to attend the Wayne Dyer seminar, *Divine Love*. This seminar is unique in that Wayne Dyer will be the only speaker for the whole two days. His books and videos have been instrumental in helping me find the strength to navigate the last few years. I am hoping this conference will center me, help jumpstart my writing process and help me deal with my grief.

We are staying at the hotel where the seminar is being held so that Kate can easily find me if she needs anything. I wake up before sunrise for the first day. The hotel warned me that attendees get in line early. I am one of the first fifty people to queue up, so I have my pick of seats once I make my way into the auditorium. I choose a seat near the aisle in the middle of the room about six rows back. I want to be as close to the stage as possible to soak up every word.

After a short while, two women sit next to me

and introduce themselves. They are sisters from Washington state. One of the women is a self-published author, and her sister has recently retired from a long career in public relations. Over the course of the morning, they share a story with me about losing their younger sister and how I remind them of her. We bond over our stories, and they instantly become my adopted sisters. We talk easily as if we have always known each other. By the end of the seminar, I have nothing but love in my heart for these two incredible women.

On the last day of the conference, I have an experience that solidifies my commitment to writing a book. Each day during the conference, we meditate in the morning and afternoon for about ten to fifteen minutes. I have tried to meditate on more than one occasion with little success. I cannot seem to quiet the little voices in my head for any measurable length of time. But this afternoon is different. I sit perfectly still and begin to focus on the tingly feeling I get when I connect with universal energy. I picture the bright yellow, gold, orange and magenta light as it enters my chest and fills my heart. I am detaching from my body and just experiencing the vastness that is the universe. I am at absolute peace. Suddenly, both of my hands begin moving back and forth in a rhythmic motion. I am startled. I try to stop my hands from moving, but the harder I try to stop them, the quicker they move. My eyes are closed, but outside my body I can see a faceless woman sitting at a desk. She is wearing a black dress with lace and ruffled sleeves. The dress is vintage, as if it is from the 1900s. As this vision becomes clearer, my right hand stops moving, but my left hand continues as if I am writing. All of a sudden, I realize this woman is me in a previous life. The universe is opening the window to my past, so that I can realize my future. I have been an author in a previous life. Emotion envelopes me, and tears begin to stream down my cheeks. The universe is showing me exactly what I should be doing, and I have salty drops of gratitude for it. I have no doubts now that writing a book is what I need to do.

***

Kate and I enjoy a wonderful organic dinner in Lahaina, and I share my decision with her about writing a book. I tell her about Vince speaking to me at the Reiki session, the women I met at the seminar and my vision of myself in a previous life as an author. "I feel as if everything in my life is propelling me to share my story of forgiving your father," I say. "After all, if I can forgive your father and care for him until the end, maybe I can inspire other people to forgive."

"I think it's a really good idea," Kate says.

"But I know it is really *our* story," I continue. "Are you comfortable with me talking about our experiences with your father's illness and his death?"

"Yes, I think this is what you were meant to do."

"You and James will have a chance to read the book before it is published."

She smiles. "I trust you to tell our story."

CHAPTER SIX

FEBRUARY — MONTH OF MEMORIES

"Losing a loved one leaves a heartache no one can heal, but their loving memory is a precious gift that no one can steal."
— Rubyanne

This month finds all three of us remembering Vince and dealing with our grief and emotions in very different ways. The choppy sea of emotions can be overwhelming for some, and grief doesn't follow a specific plan or timeline.

When grieving is unsupported, it can turn into dysthymia, a mild form of depression. Those who can't get past their grief may slide into a deeper depression marked by feelings of hopelessness and inadequacy. There is no escaping the grief process. Death is a natural part of the circle of life. Whether we choose to suffer or carry on is up to us. The danger lies in allowing grief to become a way of life.

Vince's spirit still visits Kate, but other spirits have begun visiting her, as well. At night her room is the meeting ground for multiple spirits, which is very disconcerting to a teenager. She has trouble sleeping in her room, and most nights she crawls into bed with me. She often feels Vince's spirit nearby, and finds that comforting. However, some nights, anxiety and sadness fill her. I am aware of her need for order, stability and security. We spend many nights talking about the future. Through these talks, I am able to help her focus on moving forward with her life.

We reminisce about the past with Vince. I encourage her to talk about her emotions. It is important to allow her to feel how she feels, and acknowledge her pain. She is experiencing many emotions: sadness, abandonment, fear, anxiety, heartache and anger. As she remembers her history with Vince, I try to help her refocus her thoughts on the positive memories.

"I wish Dad would have spent more time with me when I was little. I don't really have many memories of him."

"Your dad traveled all the time for his job. For your father, making a lot of money to provide a nice lifestyle for you was important," I explain. "He grew up without a lot of money, and I think he did not want you and James to feel poor like he did. Do you remember when your dad use to take you on Sundays to ride the ponies around the ring while he walked with you?"

"Kind of. I was really little."

"Your father wanted you and James to have opportunities and advantages that he and I did not have growing up. So he focused on work. He knew I was at home taking really good care of you. I hope the time you spent with him at the end helped you get to know him better."

"I think he really enjoyed our afternoon ice teas from Starbucks."

I smile. "That was the highlight of his day, Kate." Peace washes over her face. Part of her grief process will be the acceptance of who her father was to her.

***

James is handling his grief in a much different fashion. Tonight I receive a phone call from him very late in the evening. He is upset. James has done an excellent job of moving forward, but has only now started to deal with his emotions.

James and Kate were never close with their father in their early childhood, and after the divorce, Vince was even less involved. When we were all living together, I hoped that Vince would take the time to engage with the children each day. Before his diagnosis, Vince had lost his job, so he was home during the day unless he was at chemotherapy or radiation. Initially when we moved in, Vince would help organize dinner and spend time watching TV with Kate and me. After a few months, he went back to his old self, trying to control everything and driving everyone away in the process. Vince did not make it easy for the kids to connect with him. However, Kate worked at finding a way to connect. During their afternoon ice teas, She would let his criticisms roll right off of her. She knew he would not be around much longer, and she was willing to make an effort to connect.

Things were different with James. He still harbored resentment and ill feelings toward Vince for our divorce and for Vince's lack of fathering. James' call this evening is difficult to hear.

"Hey, buddy."

"Hi, Mom."

His voice is filled with anguish, remorse and regret.

"I'm having a really hard time tonight," he continues. "Why didn't I listen to you when you would tell me to spend time with Dad? Why did I go out every night with my friends instead of staying home with him? Now he is gone."

My knee-jerk reaction when one of my children is in pain, is to make it better. But anguish is part of life. All I can do is empathize with him.

"You did what felt right for you at the time. I know how much you must miss him." I try to comfort him, but I know he needs more than I can offer. James is also aware that he needs more than just a supportive phone call with me.

"I think I would like to talk to a therapist," he says.

"That's a very smart idea. Sometimes we need an outsider's perspective to help us process difficult emotions."

Seeking outside help is a very important step in the grief process. Having a professional provide you with tools to handle your grief can be incredibly beneficial. While friends and family can empathize, sometimes they are too close to the loss to be of significant help. I am so pleased that James is moving through his grief and is brave enough to ask for help.

***

I am struggling with how to begin writing the book about our journey together as a family, but the universe sends me help one morning. A good friend of mine knows a woman who helps authors with the writing process. She conducts a one-day workshop for a select group of writers once a year. My friend calls her up and tells her about the book I plan to write. Usually the workshop focuses on business writers, but the writing coach agrees to allow me to attend.

I park my car at my office and walk to the train, which will take me downtown. On the platform, I snuggle deeper into my winter coat and sip tea from a large paper cup. Nervous excitement courses through my body, but the little gremlins in my mind are attempting to undermine me. They spew self-doubt, reminding me that I have no business trying to write a book. I am not an author. The chatter in my mind will not stop.

Who do you think you are? You are going to embarrass yourself. Do you really have a story worth telling?

I walk the few short blocks from the train and navigate my way to the office building and small conference room that we will use for the day. There are several authors already seated at the table. Before I have a chance to introduce myself, the facilitator strolls in and asks everyone to take a seat. There are twelve authors all together. Today's workshop is an overview to help jumpstart the writing process. The facilitator discusses publishing options and how to build an author brand. There is a lot of information to absorb. I take volumes of notes.

Halfway through our morning, we are asked to share our book idea with the group. I am nervous.

What if my story is not worthy of being told? What if the facilitator thinks I'm not capable of writing a book or the other authors think my idea is rubbish?

Several authors have shared their book ideas and some are realizing they will either need to change focus, narrow in on a subject or hire a ghostwriter.

It is my turn. I tell the story of how I had moved in with my ex and how I want to now inspire others to find forgiveness in their lives and to share valuable information about what it's like when a loved one dies at home.

The authors are silent.

Then, suddenly the room erupts all at once.

"What an amazing story," one author says.

"This definitely has screenplay opportunities," adds another.

"I see a series of books."

"You are an inspiration."

The conversation continues for a while. With all the positive reinforcement, I know I am on the right path. I am more determined than ever to write my book. At lunch, I continue to talk with the group about the possibilities, and my excitement grows. I can't wait to start writing.

We return to the conference room to craft our book outlines. Just a few months ago, a friend shared a business organization tool with me called "mind-mapping." It is a way to stay organized by creating a "to-do" list by capturing items in a circular pattern. It transcends the linear thought process, which can break creativity for some people. The first time I saw this idea, it resonated with me. It allows me to view ideas from a distance. Ironically, we are given a similar concept to outline our books.

Next, I develop a working title and begin breaking the book into chapters. I immediately visualize each chapter and fill in notes about what stories it will encompass. The next two hours whiz by. At the end of the afternoon, we go around the room sharing our book's titles, a few chapter titles and what our books will entail. Once again, as the conversation reaches me, the authors have plenty of feedback. They challenge me to think of this manuscript as the first book in a series. I am stunned. I am still wrapping my hands around the idea of writing the first one.

As we finish our day, I am floating. I had such angst about this workshop. It turned out to be exactly what I needed to help me start the writing process. I step onto the city sidewalk. Even though it is February in Chicago, the sun is shining brightly. I wrap my scarf around my neck, pull my gloves on and happily walk to the train station just a few blocks away. What an amazing and productive experience. On the train ride speeding home, I can feel Vince's spirit nearby encouraging me. I am aware in this moment that I am moving on past my grief. I am grateful for my experiences with Vince, good and bad. They have led me to this moment. Those experiences will help me inspire others.

***

The next day I begin writing *Walking Toward the Light: A journey in forgiveness and death.* I wake each morning around three to write for four or five hours before Kate wakes up. The house is so quiet, and the words flow out of my fingers onto the keyboard without hesitation. Some days, reliving the memories is difficult, but I know that by recalling them I am also letting go of the emotions that I have attached to them. I am letting go of the pain and I am forgiving once again.

I have decided to self publish my first book. I know searching for a book agent or finding a publisher can take a couple of years. Literary agents receive hundreds of books each week to consider for representation. Breaking through the clutter on their desks is nearly impossible. Nowadays it is relatively simple to self publish. The key is finding a strong editor.

As the month draws to a close, I have completed my first draft of my book and have also selected a cover design. I am feeling blessed and happy. My grief is diminishing, and in its place is possibility.

CHAPTER SEVEN

MARCH — LIFE MOVES ON

"In three words I can sum up everything I've learned about life: IT GOES ON."
—Robert Frost

March is the month that high school seniors begin receiving their acceptance or rejection letters from colleges. A large thick envelope means an acceptance package and a smaller envelope or thinner package generally means a rejection or deferral. Kate has already received two large packages. She was accepted to the University of South Carolina, her father's alma mater, and the University of Indiana. She is eagerly awaiting news from SMU in Dallas.

It is dark when I head to the mailbox. Many of Kate's friends received notices today from their schools. As I open the mailbox, I see the thick, red envelope with a blue horse embossed on the cover. I shriek out loud. I can hardly contain my excitement as I run back to the house. I set the rest of the mail on the counter and close my eyes, wondering if Vince is here this evening.

I run up the stairs two at a time to Kate's room.

"You've got mail," I shout.

She smiles and takes the envelope from my hands. She carefully slides out the contents and reads the first sentence of the letter.

"Dear Katherine, we are pleased to welcome you to…"

Tears roll down my cheeks as I beam with pride. I can't help but throw my arms around her and squeeze her tight. Through all the turmoil of Vince's passing during the past year, she has managed to keep her focus on school and college. Her commitment has paid off.

"I am so proud of you," I tell her.

"Do you think Dad is here? Do you think he knows?" Kate asks.

It is in these moments that I am filled with sorrow for Kate—and for Vince. He will miss every single milestone.

"Yes. I'm sure he knows, and he is so very proud of you."

Vince and I both attended colleges that were affordable for our families and easy to get into. Applying to college in the late seventies and early eighties was much different than it is today. Back when I applied for college, I filled out a two-page form and wrote a one-page essay. Nowadays, applying requires toiling over a lengthy application online, and writing a long essay. Families often hire coaches to proof their child's essay to make sure it is unique and meets the requirements of the university.

I sit on the edge of Kate's bed as she begins to look through all the papers in the packet.

"Do you think we should send in my housing deposit so that I am first on the list for the best dorm?" she asks.

"Absolutely."

"But I haven't heard from my first choice college yet. Should I wait?"

"You won't hear from them until May. Let's send in a deposit just to make sure we secure a place for you until you decide."

Somehow I know she will be attending SMU.

I walk down the hall to my bedroom, and I am aware of Vince's spirit standing near me. I smile as tears of joy slide down my cheeks yet again. I can feel his pride in her accomplishment. Vince and I always wanted our children to be able to attend colleges that he and I had only dreamt of attending.

***

James is halfway through his second semester. He is enjoying the freedom of living on his own and the autonomy to create his own goals. He problem-solves and manages his life without relying on me at all. Our relationship has grown over the past few months, and I can feel our mother-son bond growing. He has been through so much with Vince's death, and he is finding his path and moving on in a healthy way.

***

Feelings of grief return to me as I begin accepting that my father will die soon. He was diagnosed in October with non-alcoholic cirrhosis of the liver. Generally cirrhosis of the liver is a scarring of the liver caused by years of alcohol abuse or hepatitis. The liver is an essential organ responsible for detoxifying harmful substances in your body, cleaning your blood and making vital nutrients. My father's cirrhosis is hereditary; he is the third sibling of ten to suffer with symptoms from cirrhosis of the liver, for which there is no cure. At the time of his diagnosis, he was given six months to live, and that time is passing quickly.

He has begun sleeping much more and is growing weaker as the days wear on. I have decided it is time to see my father one last time. While his death is not imminent, I want to see him while he is still lucid and able to speak to me. Because I have been through this process with Vince recently, I can see the signs that my father's body is beginning to slow down.

He has asked to see the grandchildren one last time. While I understand my father's wish, I also know it may be too soon for the children to emotionally deal with more death. I call James to share the news with him and ask him if he is up to visiting Grampy.

My children have always called my father Grampy and my mother Mimi. When I had James, my mother was just forty-five years old, and she felt too young to be called Grandma. So we chose Mimi, and my father selected the endearing name of Grampy.

"I just don't think I can see Grampy sick," James says. "It's too soon after Dad's death for me. I am really sorry."

"I understand. I thought that might be the case."

"Will you call me from there so I can talk to everyone?"

"Absolutely. Love you, buddy."

"Love you, too."

I am completely supportive of James' decision. He has worked very hard to move through his grief, and the reality is that my children have never been close with my parents. I am in agreement that he remain behind and not derail all the progress he has made.

I am surprised when Kate agrees to make the trip with me. I am worried that seeing my father ill might be difficult for her. We were fortunate that Vince looked almost healthy until the day he passed. He never appeared sickly and was not bedridden until the last week of his life. This made his passing so much easier on James and Kate.

I have no idea what my father looks like. My mom is still in denial about his condition and that he will die soon. I know firsthand that as a primary caretaker it can also be difficult to see the changes occurring because they happen so gradually. But, I can hear the strain in my mom's voice each time we talk.

The toxins have begun to build up in my father's brain, and he now takes medication several times a day to eliminate the poisons from his body. Unfortunately, one of the side effects from this medicine is the constant elimination of his bowels. He is unstable when he walks, so he often does not make it to the bathroom in time. But my father is a trooper, and he knows if he does not take this medicine that ultimately the toxins will build up. Once that occurs, he will have to be hospitalized. I don't want to put any additional strain on my parents by staying with them, so we arrange to stay at a nearby hotel. I am hoping that our visit will help lift my mother's spirits.

***

It is Saturday night, the night before we are flying to California to visit my parents. Kate and I will be sandwiching a two-day visit in between other obligations we both have. Kate sheepishly enters my room and climbs up onto my bed. My suitcase is open and I am packing.

"Is everything okay?" I ask.

She nods her head yes, but I know differently.

I can tell there is something wrong, and I think I know what it is.

"What's wrong?"

"Nothing."

"How are you feeling about seeing Grampy?"

All at once Kate begins to sob.

"I don't think I can go. I just don't think I can handle seeing Grampy sick. It's too soon."

I hug her tightly.

"I'm afraid I am disappointing you and Mimi."

I push my suitcase aside, climb into bed with her and hold her in my arms.

"I was worried it would be too soon for you. That's why James is not going. It's too soon for him. You know everyone will understand. You have been through a lot, and no one will be hurt if you don't go to California." I look her in the eyes before I continue. "You know, Kate, a really important skill to have as an adult is to know what you need and to ask for it. I'm happy you are being honest with me about how you're feeling."

Of course, I am a little disappointed. Not in Kate but in the situation. I was really looking forward to having her with me to take my mind off the fact that I am losing my father. But I am the adult. Kate should be allowed to process losing her father so she can move on with her life. Her grief is beyond anything I will experience when I lose my father. I am an adult who has had the opportunity to spend a lifetime with him.

I am concerned about leaving Kate alone while she is sad, so I call my best friend's sister to see if she can stay with her for two nights while I am away. She is more than happy to help. I feel better knowing Kate will have an adult with her in the evenings if she needs to talk.

I head to the airport the next morning to catch my flight. My mother does not know that Kate will not be coming with me yet, and I am anxious to tell her. I know she will be sad. I am walking to the gate thinking of what to say to her when I see a very good friend waiting to board a different airplane.

"Hi," I say.

"Hi." She reaches over and hugs me very hard. "Where are you going?"

"Heading to California to visit my father. He has asked me to come visit one last time."

Her arms wrap around me once again.

The gate agent gives the boarding call for her flight.

"Please give my love to your family. I know what a tough time this is for all of you. I'll call you when I am back in town, and we will get together."

I smile. She has no idea how much our brief interaction just meant to me. I needed a hug, and she was there. I have never once bumped into her at the airport, and we both travel frequently. Isn't it funny how the universe has a way of sending you what you need at exactly the perfect time?

I walk to my gate and stand nearby so I can hear the announcements. I call my mother ready to share the news with her that Kate will not be coming with me. I am worried she will be disappointed, but my mother handles the news much better than I anticipated. She understands that the visit would be very hard on Kate.

I board the plane for the four-hour flight, excited to see my mother and sad knowing that I will be saying goodbye to my father. I have rented a car, so my mother is not burdened with picking me up at the airport. I arrive in the early afternoon and drive to my parents' house.

My mother is pale and hunched over. She is clearly stressed and taxed from caring for my father. I hug her tightly and walk inside to find my father lying on the sofa. I walk over and bend down to hug him. His skin is pale, and he looks much older than when I last saw him in December. His stomach is swollen, and he is now growing a mustache. It looks completely out of place because he is now bald. He wears a long-sleeve shirt to cover all the bruises on his arms from his blood-thinning medication.

"Hi, Dad."

He sits up slowly, and my mother is immediately at his side asking if he needs anything. She has been working a full-time job from 6 a.m. to 2:30 p.m., five days a week. My mother is young, just sixty-six years old, and has decided to work as long as she possibly can. She enjoys having a purpose and will continue to work even after my father's passing. Her company has allowed her to have a flexible schedule so she can care for my father. When he has difficult days, she works from home. Many evenings while he sleeps peacefully, she will stay up until midnight completing work so she does not fall behind. Some day soon, as my father requires more and more care, she will begin using the vacation time she has saved up over the past year to stay home.

She is exhausted working full-time, preparing meals for the both of them and taking care of my father's needs. I spend the afternoon and evening with them until my father goes to sleep around seven. I head to my hotel, feeling strange that I am not staying with my parents. I originally thought it would be too much of a strain on them to have both Kate and me staying there, especially with the side effects from his new medication. I ask my mom to call me the next morning when they are up and ready for me to come over.

I head to the hotel to check in. I am exhausted and order a grilled chicken sandwich and beer for dinner. Before I climb into bed for a tranquil night's sleep, I check in with Kate and update her on Grampy's condition. Kate reminds me how I will be able to help my mother with Grampy's death because I have been through this before. I am grateful to be alone when the tears start to fall.

***

In the morning, I catch a quick workout in the hotel gym. I am still exhausted and hope that the rush of adrenaline from my workout will energize me. Just as I am getting out of the shower, my mom calls and invites me over.

My father grew up in South Carolina where grits were a morning staple. He continued the tradition in our home when I was a child. I arrive just in time for a breakfast of grits, tomatoes and scrambled eggs, and my tummy enjoys the reminder of my youth.

I spend the rest of the day with my parents. At one point, there is a discussion of my father wanting a heated blanket. He is always cold. He keeps the house at seventy-eight degrees, so it feels almost like a sauna. I decide to go purchase one for his side of the bed. My mother could use a break, so I suggest she join me on an outing while my father sleeps.

As we drive to the store, I take the opportunity to check in with her.

"How are you doing?" I ask. She looks pale and tired.

"Your dad had a good night. He only got up once," she says.

"Okay, but I asked how you are doing—not how Dad is doing."

She turns to me with a blank look.

"You look tired, Mom, and I am worried that you aren't eating enough."

"I'm fine. Your Dad is actually doing really good. I think this new medicine is really helping him."

It is easy when you are a full-time caregiver to become immune to the gradual deteriorations that accompany terminal illness. I can see a major difference in my father's body and mind since December, but my mom claims my father has improved.

"I'm worried about you juggling work and caring for Dad as he continues to grow weaker," I say. "You look exhausted, and I can see the strain it's placed on you. Maybe it would be good to start letting some people help you?"

We park the car and make our way inside to the department store.

She ignores my previous statement. "So your dad wants a heated baby blanket."

"I'm pretty sure there is no such thing as a heated baby blanket. That would be dangerous."

"Well, let's look. Your dad is adamant about wanting just a small baby blanket that is heated."

"I remember when Vince would ask for things that didn't make sense. It's almost like you are negotiating with a child. And if you say 'no,' he'll just become more agitated."

My mom slowly turns to look at me. "Yes. It's so hard."

"You have to remember that you are the adult and caregiver and that you will need to begin making decisions to keep Dad safe when he can't reason for himself. I know you are used to Dad making all the decisions, but there will be times when he is making choices with the intellect of a child."

We find the heated blankets in the department store.

"You know, sometimes he wakes up at night and looks just like a little boy and even talks like a child."

I place my hand over hers. "It's going to get harder."

Tears spring to her eyes. "I don't know if I'm going to be able to handle much more."

"I think it is time to get hospice involved. They are such a great support system."

"Your dad isn't dying yet," she says.

I have said too much. Her denial has returned, but I know I need to begin preparing her.

"You know, everyone thinks you call hospice at the very end when death is just days away, but that's not true. We called hospice before Vince was really sick in March, and he did not pass until September. They were a great resource as his health began to decline. They took care of ordering any medical equipment we needed. They had his prescriptions delivered to our door every week. Just that little bit of help took some pressure off of me."

I can see her thinking about what I have just said, and I don't want to overwhelm her.

"So I think we should buy a heated twin-size blanket, and we can put it on Dad's side of the bed," I say. "Then you can turn it on a half hour before he is going to bed to warm up the sheets for him. Then turn it down very low as he sleeps."

"So you don't think they have any heated baby blankets?" she asks. "Maybe we should ask someone."

"Let's just buy this one. I'm pretty sure we are not going to be able to find a baby blanket. This will be better, because it's for an adult. I will explain it to Dad."

We pay and silently make our way to the car.

"I know how scared you must be and how frustrating it is to live in limbo," I say.

"I keep asking the doctors to tell me how much longer he has, and no one will tell me."

"No one, not even the doctors can be sure when the end will come, Mom. They are not going to be able to give you a date. You know they gave him six months in October. I know he is fighting to hang on to make it to your fiftieth wedding anniversary next month."

"He sleeps a lot," she says. "In fact I think he sleeps all day while I am at work."

"The last month of Vince's life, he slept most of the day, too. It was hard because then at night he would be up every couple of hours."

"Yes! That's exactly what happens with your father. But he is not himself most of the time."

"I remember how hard it is to step in and begin making the decisions," I say. "I know you are used to having Dad's input. Soon you will need to assume the role of the one in charge. He will become weaker and less coherent, and you will need to stay home with him full time for his own safety. He will begin functioning with the mental capacity of a child because of the toxins in his brain, and you will need to be firm with him for his own safety. I think it would be great to get hospice involved, so they will be in the loop when you need to start staying home full time."

I glance at her to gauge her reaction before I continue.

"There will come a time when you will be unable to leave the house or even the room, because Dad will need constant supervision. I can see Dad's energy waning. Hospice can help you through the transition when Dad is no longer mobile. They can order the hospital bed and any other equipment and medication you may need."

"I just feel like it's not time yet," she says. "He is doing really good now with this new medication."

"It's not about it being time for him to go; it's about getting help in place for when you need it.

Dad's needs may change quickly, and then you will be left scrambling to enlist hospice."

She nods her head slowly. "I will call them tomorrow."

"I promise that you calling hospice will be the best thing you do. They will be a great support for you as Dad's health declines."

"When do you think he will die?" she asks.

"I don't know. No one can say for sure. I do know he is much worse than he was in December."

Her eyes fill with tears. "I'll call hospice tomorrow."

I encourage all families dealing with a terminal illness where the patient wants to die at home to connect with hospice as soon as possible. Many families think that if they call hospice it means their family member is dying. In our case with Vince, we began with palliative care, which provides specialized medical care for people with long-term illnesses. It focuses on providing relief for patients from the pain and stress of a long-term illness such as cancer. This can help improve the quality of life not only for the patient but for the entire family, as well. Families are also often reticent to involve hospice because they are worried their dying family member will think they are giving up on them. Hospice caregivers are trained to deal with end-of-life scenarios. They provide comfort both to the patient and to the family members, helping them transition through the many stages before death comes.

I spend the rest of the afternoon sitting in the living room watching my father sleep while the TV plays yet another reality show. I am shocked at how many reality shows are on TV, the only TV my father watches.

He wakes in the afternoon and struggles to sit up on the sofa. The cushions are soft and there is no support. He barely has the energy to pull himself up, but he is insistent that he lie on the sofa to sleep during the day. As he sits up, he looks at me with a child-like expression.

"I'm hungry," he announces just like a little kid. "What are we having for lunch?"

"What would you like?" I ask.

"Pizza," he says.

My mother rushes in. "Everything okay?"

"Yes. Dad was just saying he wants pizza for lunch."

"Lunch? I want pizza for dinner. It's dinner time." His voice is gruff.

"Okay, no problem," my mom says. You want pepperoni?"

"Yes." He lies down and goes back to sleep.

I can see she is troubled with the exchange we have just had, so I follow her into the kitchen. "You seem upset. Is everything okay?" I ask.

She is on the verge of tears. "Everything is fine. It's just that I can tell the toxins are building up again in your dad's brain. He hasn't taken his medicine since you have been here because he did not want to have an accident and embarrass himself."

"Mom, that's why I stayed in a hotel, so I would not create any stress."

"I know, but he was worried about the days. He is difficult to control at night when he is not taking his medication for the toxins. I can tell he is getting confused and agitated. I am worried that tonight is going to be really hard."

I place my arm around her shoulder. "I will stay with you tonight and help you with Dad. I can take care of him so you can get some sleep."

"I'm fine. I don't want you not sleeping. You have to fly home tomorrow."

"I am so sorry I can't stay longer. James comes home from school Wednesday. I can sleep on the plane. I'll go check out of the hotel so I can stay here tonight with you."

"Can you do that? Check out early?"

"Sure. It won't be a problem."

"Why don't I go over now while dad is sleeping and then I can pick up a pizza on my way back?"

"Can I come with you?"

"Sure. Will Dad be all right on his own?"

"Yes. He will sleep for a couple of hours now."

We arrive at the hotel, and I stop at the front desk to explain my situation to the manager. I use this hotel frequently when I visit my parents, so they are happy to allow me to check out early. We take the elevator to my room, and my mother sits on my bed as I begin repacking my suitcase.

"This bed is really comfortable," she says.

"I know, right?"

"Are you sure you went to check out? This bed is way more comfortable than the guest bed at my house."

I smile at her. "Maybe you should stay at the hotel tonight so you can enjoy the comfy bed?"

She smiles back, and for a moment she has some relief from the stress of being my father's caregiver.

Fortunately, the night is uneventful and everyone gets a good night's sleep. I spend the next morning with my parents watching more reality TV.

I feel very strange. My father and I have not spoken very much on this trip because he has been sleeping so much. I am uncomfortable knowing that this will most likely be the last time I see my father. I feel like I should be saying something profound, but words escape me as the reality of the situation sinks in.

***

My departure time arrives, and my father insists on walking me to the door. He uses a cane and is very unstable. We both know this is the last time we will see each other. We both know this is goodbye, but the lump in my throat won't allow anything more than, "I love you."

"I love you, too," he says and gives me a hug.

My mom walks me to the car, and I hug her tightly. I am filled with emotion I keep buried. I must be strong for her.

"You call me anytime. I'm always here for you," I remind her.

"I know."

"I mean it. If you need anything, call and I will get here as fast as I can."

I climb into the car and drive away, I am left feeling so unsettled and disappointed in myself. I should have said more to my father. He was the best father he could be, and I never doubted that he loved me. As I drive to the airport, I know that my emotions are raw and too fresh on the heels of Vince's passing just five months earlier. My sadness and fear kept me from saying the things I should have said to him.

Maybe I should write a letter saying all the things I so desperately wanted to say.

I seek solace knowing I said the most important thing to him: "I love you."

CHAPTER EIGHT

APRIL — FAMILY TIES

"A mother's love for her child is like nothing else in the world. It knows no law, no pity, it dares all things and crushes down remorselessly all that stands in its path."
— Agatha Christie

Some days it feels as if Vince has just died. Still other days it seems as if he has been gone for much longer than six months.

Kate will be returning home from her spring break trip today. I am expecting her within the hour, so I head upstairs to shower after my long workout. I have been listening to upbeat club music for my run, so I decide to switch to a more subdued Van Morrison playlist. I am playing the music from my iPhone through a wireless speaker perched in an alcove next to the sink in the master bathroom. It's a cute little speaker about four inches wide and three inches tall. It fits perfectly on the wide shelf. *Brown Eyed Girl* plays through the speaker as I sing along. Suddenly, I hear a loud bang. I open the shower door to see what has fallen. As I look around the room, I see the speaker sitting in the sink. I am confused. There is no way that little speaker could have flipped off the alcove area. Suddenly, a light bulb goes out above the mirror, and I can feel Vince's energy in the room. *Brown Eyed Girl* was our song. We both loved Van Morrison, and Vince always referred to me as his brown-eyed girl.

Kate arrives home just a few moments later. I point to the speaker.

"What happened?" she asks.

"It fell off into the sink."

She smiles at me. "Dad is here. It's Easter, and he wants to make sure I know he is thinking about me."

She scampers off to her room. I am in awe of how well she continues to handle her grief and Vince's death. I know in these moments when she feels his presence, that she is comforted.

Kate and I are preparing to travel to Paris and Italy this month. It was Vince's wish that Kate and I go to Europe as a graduation gift. A reward to Kate for a job well done.

We will spend five days in Paris and then ten days in Italy touring several cities. We will end our trip in Milan where we will meet up with several members of Vince's family, including his mother and sister-in-law. Next we travel to Trento for time with Vince's mother's relatives. Shortly after, I will depart, and Kate will stay on with Vince's family for another three weeks.

It has been a juggling act to coordinate everyone's schedules. We are trying to work the trip around events like a surgery Vince's brother is having, my parent's fiftieth wedding anniversary and Kate's graduation at the end of May. Even though she finished senior year early, Kate will receive her diploma with her class. As always, I acquiesce to Vince's family's needs and move the schedule around to accommodate his brother's surgery. This means I will miss my parents' anniversary. Even with my father's terminal diagnosis, he was determined to make it to their fiftieth, a major milestone for any couple. I feel incredibly guilty for missing this event, but Vince's brother's surgery has been scheduled and cannot be moved.

Kate and I depart for Paris on the evening of April 17th. We are giddy with the anticipation of traveling in Europe together. I have always dreamt of visiting Paris, and I am so thrilled to be there with my daughter.

As we board the airplane and take our seats, I am filled with such gratitude. We have both been through a lot in the last year, and I am delighted we are able to have this time together. The overnight flight will be nine hours, and we will arrive in Paris the following morning. We settle in for the long flight and begin making plans for the next day. We excitedly discuss what foods we want to eat while in Paris and all of the sights we want to see.

"Dad didn't visit me last night," Kate says. "I thought he would come see me last night to wish me well."

"You seem disappointed?" I say.

"Yes." She turns her attention to her meal.

It takes all my strength to not jump in and justify or explain what might have happened. As a parent you never want to see your children in pain. All I want to do is take away her anguish, but I know that would be wrong. Learning to process pain is an important life skill. She is beginning to feel separated from Vince, and this is a natural part of the grief process. I have learned the hard way over the years that rushing in to minimize or remove suffering from your children strips them of the opportunity to grow, mature and develop coping mechanisms. I reach over and gently place my hand on her arm and smile at her. This little bit of comfort is all I can offer her during her grief.

***

We arrive in Paris the next morning and enjoy a cappuccino outside on the hotel patio while we wait for our room to be prepared. We are both tired from the long flight and are desperate to take a shower.

We spend the next five days in Paris soaking up time together. I am struggling to rebuild my business, but am fortunate that I can work from anywhere as long as there is internet access. I know I will never get this time back with her, so I am committed to relishing each and every moment. In August, she will leave for college, and I have a suspicion that she will rarely be home. Kate is incredibly independent and has a zest for traveling and experiencing life. She has big hopes and dreams. She reminds me so much of myself at her age.

Our five days in Paris go by quickly. We are having trouble adjusting to Paris time, so we sleep late in the mornings and walk around the city in the afternoons. We savor many amazing meals, including a three-hour lunch one rainy afternoon at *Le Jules Verne* in the Eiffel Tower. We drink champagne and wine paired with course after course of delicious French cuisine. The highlight of the meal is the chocolate soufflés paired with an amazing dessert wine.

The following evening, Kate and I are at dinner and the conversation turns to Vince for a while. We spend time reminiscing about him. She continues to ask questions about his life and why he did not leave a letter for her.

"You know, I am really upset that he didn't leave me a letter like I asked," she says.

"I know."

We've had the same conversation before, so I try a different route.

"Maybe I can share some stories with you. What do you want to know?" I ask.

"Why was he so mean to me sometimes? He used to tell me I had no common sense."

I try to think of a way to explain Vince's background to Kate. I know it has a lot to do with Vince's own upbringing, so I remind Kate of her paternal grandfather, whom she called Pop-pop.

"I know your father was not the best father in the world, but he had a very difficult childhood." I say. "Pop-pop was not a very good role model for your dad. When your dad was little, Pop-pop used to make fun of him and belittle him. If your father did something wrong, Pop-pop used to beat him with his fists."

Kate's eyes open wide. "That's terrible. I really don't remember Pop-pop. I was so little when he died."

"Yes. You were just three years old when he passed away. Pop-pop became a different man after you and James were born. But before he had grandchildren, he was an angry man, and he was a horrible father to your father. Pop-pop never showed love to your father as a child, so your dad really didn't learn how to show love as a father. I know he loves you and James very much. He worked hard his entire life saving money, so when he retired he could enjoy spending time with you and James. I think the older you got the more comfortable he got spending time with you. I think he was looking forward to spending time with you as adults. Unfortunately, time ran out."

"That's sad," Kate says.

"I'm not telling you that I am condoning your father's actions. He should have tried to spend more time with you and James and to be more caring. I always tried to be a really good mom to make up for anything you lacked from your father. But you need to know his actions came from a place of brokenness. He did not mean to be callous. His actions had nothing to do with you personally or his love for you."

This is a lot for a seventeen-year-old to take in, but I want her to find forgiveness so she can move on. Vince is gone, and the past is in the past. I can tell Kate misses her father. She became close to him during the time we lived together. She made an effort to meet him on his own terms and make time for him. That made living together as a family absolutely worth all the effort.

"I think he has stopped visiting me," she says. "I wonder if he will visit me while we are in Italy?"

"I'm not sure his passport is valid," I joke.

We both giggle as we finish sipping our champagne.

We end our Paris trip with a dinner cruise on the river Seine. We are fortunate to have a table at the bow of the boat with great views of all the architecture along the shoreline. The sun sets, and the city comes alive with the lights and energy of the night. The highlight is the view of the Eiffel Tower. Just as the boat nears this amazing structure it goes dark and then suddenly it lights up with millions of tiny white lights. It is a spectacular sight that takes my breath away. I am overcome with joy and grateful to be in Paris with Kate.

***

From Paris we travel to Rome, Positano, and then Milan, where we will meet Vince's family. Positano is a beautiful seaside town on the western coast of Italy. We are staying at the only hotel located right on the beach. We have a lovely terrace overlooking the Tyrrhenian Sea. We spend our days bathing in the sun and shopping the boutiques that line the cobblestone streets. Kate and I fall in love with Positano. We could have stayed for weeks. Fortunately, it is raining the morning we depart, making it a little easier for us to bid goodbye.

Our next stop will be Milan, where we will spend two days together before Vince's mother and sister-in-law arrive.

***

When Vince's family arrives, we are elated to be in Italy together. There are lots of hugs, smiles and much excitement. We meet in the bar for cocktails and snacks. The highlight of our Milan stay is our last night. Kate and I host a family dinner at *il Savini* in the *Galleria Vittorio Emanuele II.* We dined there for lunch one rainy afternoon before everyone arrived, and we are determined to bring Vince's family back there for dinner. The night air is mild, and we enjoy a pleasant evening dining on the portico. My mother-in-law laughs as we share family stories. It almost feels like old times.

We have all weathered Vince's passing and now are in Italy celebrating Kate's graduation as a family. As the evening winds down, we savor multiple courses of cheeses, meats, pastas, desserts and Prosecco and wine. Laughter, happiness and love fill the air.

***

We wake early to board the train for a three-hour ride to Verona, where we will meet up with several of Vince's relatives. The train ride is uneventful, and we chat the entire way, anticipating how wonderful it will be to see Vince's relatives again. Kate and I have met them all before some thirteen years ago.

Everyone is cheerful as our train pulls into Verona. We have just a few minutes to offload the luggage before the train departs for the next stop. In true tourist fashion, I accidentally grab another woman's suitcase. She chases me down the aisle of the train and accuses me of stealing her bag. I am so embarrassed.

Vince's family is waiting for us as we step off the platform. I am so excited to see them all again. There are hugs for Vince's mother and lots of tears and kisses. She reintroduces Kate to everyone. Kate was just four years old when we were last in Italy. My mother-in-law introduces my sister-in-law, who is in Italy for the first time. While I have met everyone ages ago, I can tell that many of them do not recognize me. Needless to say, I probably look somewhat different. I stand to the side of my mother-in-law and awkwardly wait for her to introduce me. Instead she turns her back to me and begins to speak with one of her cousins. I immediately, step up and reintroduce myself. Suddenly, I feel out of place, but I push these thoughts aside as we begin to walk toward our transportation.

It takes several vehicles and vans to accommodate all five travelers and our large bags.

We head towards Trento for a lovely lunch on the water. Everyone is as friendly as I remember, and many of them have learned to speak some English since my last visit, so conversation is much easier this time around. Unfortunately, my Italian is now worse; I have not used it since we visited more than a decade ago. After lunch, we stroll leisurely back to the vehicles and head to our hotel in Trento. I walk alongside my mother-in-law chatting about lunch and the wonderful wine we enjoyed. Her conversation with me is stilted and her answers abrupt. She does not want to engage with me, and I am curious as to what I have done wrong.

The drive through the mountainous region is spectacular. Italy never fails to take my breath away. We spend the next few days eating delectable meals and sightseeing throughout the countryside. The temperatures are so mild that we leave the windows of our hotel room open to breathe in the fresh air and enjoy the mountain views.

Throughout the next couple of days as we spend time with the family, I continue to sense distance from Vince's mother, and I am bewildered. One afternoon, I volunteer to ride in her car with one of her cousins as we make our way to our next destination. My sister-in-law has been riding with her, so I offer to switch cars. As we make our way through the countryside, Vince's mother chats away in Italian with her cousin. I listen and try to remember some Italian from our previous trip. Occasionally I jump into the conversation with a question about something we have just passed. My mother-in-law answers me abruptly with as few words as possible or ignores my question all together.

On our last evening together, the family has arranged for everyone to have dinner together at a fun pizzeria. As we stand outside waiting for everyone to arrive, I try to make conversation once again with my mother-in-law, but her answers are again short. This time I am clear she does not want to speak with me. Tonight she seems sad and withdrawn. Her grief is visible on her face. I push my own feelings of hurt aside. Her grief must be so deep, and I am worried that my presence is a reminder that Vince is gone. I begin to wonder if I should have headed back for the states earlier. But I knew it would be rude not to travel north with everyone to see Vince's extended family again.

At dinner, Kate and I are seated across the table from Vince's mother. We both struggle to make conversation with her. Kate sits to my left, and at one point excitedly discusses high school graduation with Vince's mother.

"I'm so glad you are able to come for my graduation," she says to her.

"Of course," her grandmother says.

"Just think," I say, joining in, "in four years, you will be watching her graduate from college."

She looks at me with an expressionless face. "I will be ten feet under by then. God willing."

I am shocked and don't know how to respond. The pain over the loss of her son is deep. And in this moment, I feel like my face is a reminder he is gone.

Kate's eyes fill with tears. She excuses herself from the table. Vince's mother is unaware of the wound she has just opened up in Kate.

"Where did Kate go?" she asks.

"She is upset. She just lost Vince, and I think it is hard for her to hear you talk about wanting to die," I explain.

"I didn't mean to upset her. I just know I won't be here then."

I can tell I have overstepped. "Maybe just be sensitive not to talk about your death around her. She just lost her father, and she is still learning to cope."

"Well, I lost my son."

The sting from her words feels like a hard slap across my face.

Mothers are a unique breed. We love our children unconditionally and fiercely. I cannot imagine how Vince's mother must feel. Her grief is fresh, and the reality is that death can make a person angry. It's a natural part of the grief progression. Not everyone will feel anger, but it is absolutely natural to feel it. Maybe she blames me for Vince's death. I know there is some animosity for my divorcing him.

Does she think his death is my fault because I abandoned our marriage?

I am hurt and these thoughts are upsetting to me. I put my life on hold to care for Vince until the very end. Maybe in grief you need to be angry with someone, and I am that someone. I am relieved to be leaving the next morning.

***

I am sad to be leaving Kate. I have enjoyed all of our adventures in Paris and Italy. This has been a trip of a lifetime for me. For Kate, it will be the first of many trips to Europe.

"Are you sad to be leaving?" Kate asks when she sees me packing my bags.

"Yes. I have had so much fun traveling with you. I can't believe we have been together for the last three weeks. We make a great travel team. But, I am looking forward to getting home. I have been a little uncomfortable around Nana. She doesn't talk to me, and she always seems angry at me."

"Yeah, I think she is mad Dad is gone and she is taking it out on you." Leave it to a young person to see something so clearly.

"I know," I say. "I'm sure it must be really hard for her, but I'm a little hurt. I put my life on hold for your dad, and if I didn't take care of your dad, the truth is it would have fallen on her."

"It's like you don't exist sometimes," Kate says. "You know it's weird, no one even talks to me about the fact that I have lost my father. It's like they all forget he was my dad. Everyone is always comforting Nana. She talks about death all the time. It's really depressing. Nana has never asked me how I am feeling, or even seems to care if I'm okay."

"I think because you are so stoic and you are choosing to live life instead of being mired in grief, she forgets that you have had a loss, too."

"All Nana talks about is dying. I've lost my

father, my grandfather is dying—does she think I need to hear her say she is dying?"

"I think Nana is so consumed with her grief and cannot see anything else around her. Are you going to be okay here?" I ask. "Do you feel like you want to come home?"

"No. I will be fine. I will be busy with the cousins, and I have my own room, so I can have a break when I need it."

Kate will be staying on alone in our hotel room. My mother-in-law is insistent that she stay in Kate's room. I assure her that Kate is perfectly capable of staying in her own hotel room. My mother-in-law is not happy with my decision, but Kate will be leaving for college in the fall and some independence is good for her. After all, their hotel room is just down the hall if something should happen.

The next morning I leave while it is still dark for the three hour drive to the Milan airport. I am sad to be leaving Italy. I love the lifestyle here. People really focus on quality of life and living in the moment. As we pull away from the hotel, it begins to drizzle and my thoughts turn to Vince for a moment. I wonder if Vince's spirit has been with us? My grief bubbles up. I remember our last trip to Italy as a family. Little did we know then that it would be Vince's only trip to Italy. A tear rolls down my cheek as I begin the long journey home.

CHAPTER NINE

MAY — HIS REVENGE

"There is no revenge so complete as forgiveness."
— Josh Billings

I return home to an empty house. James has just finished his first year of college and decides to stay for summer school. I am pleased he is enjoying school and working to make up for the year he deferred to spend time with Vince. He is planning to fly home for Kate's graduation at the end of the month. It has been a couple of months since I last saw him, and I have missed him.

He is working hard, as evidenced by the rise in his GPA. He has learned to do laundry, cook meals and manage his day-to-day life all on his own. He inspires me.

Several days after I arrive home, I receive a text from Kate one morning. She is sick with a low-grade fever and her glands are swollen. I am not surprised she is sick. The travel schedule while in Trento with Vince's family, such wonderful hosts, has been busy.

Each day they have activities planned from morning until night.

When Kate and I speak, I can hear the tiredness in her voice. She is fighting a virus. She reveals to me that she told Nana she is not feeling well and just wants to stay in bed today. She tells me that Nana came to her room and insisted she get dressed so she could take her to lunch and to the shops. Kate explained to her that she really is sick and she doesn't think she should go shopping. Kate loves to shop, so I know if she is turning down an afternoon of boutique hopping, she must be feeling very ill.

"I told her I just need to rest, but she said I am not sick and that I am just depressed because Dad died and his birthday is coming up. I wasn't even thinking about his birthday."

Kate's voice comes out strained and hoarse. "Nana told me to get dressed. She said shopping would make me feel better. Mom, I don't even want to get out of bed. I just want to rest," she tells me.

I am horrified that Vince's mother is pressuring Kate. I know Kate just needs someone to sympathize with her and take care of her. No matter how old we get, we all still want that to some degree when we are sick.

"Mom, she said that if I'm so sick, she'd put me on a plane home. She said she'd be back to check on me in a bit."

As Kate reiterates the entire exchange to me, I am sure she must be dramatizing the situation. I cannot believe that Vince's mother wants to send a sick child alone on a long plane ride.

"Don't worry. I will call Nana and speak with her," I say.

I hang up with Kate and dial Vince's mother.

"I'm just calling because I just spoke with Kate and I wanted to say how sorry I am that she is sick. Honestly, I'm not surprised she is. The travel schedule has been very busy, and I'm sure she is run down and fighting a virus. She should be back on her feet in twenty-four hours. This happens when she gets run down."

"Well, I was just in her room and I think she is depressed. You know, Vince's birthday is coming up in a couple of days."

Until speaking with Kate, I had forgotten that Vince's birthday was approaching. Since our divorce, it was not something I had on my calendar. I know the pending date must be upsetting to Vince's mom.

"I am pretty sure Kate is not depressed or sad," I say. "She would tell me if she was. She is sick. She has a fever."

I do not share with Vince's mother that Kate had not remembered that it was Vince's birthday.

"Well. Maybe she needs to go home then if she is so sick."

I can feel my blood pressure elevate. It is in this moment that I now see where Vince's lack of empathy and compassion has come from.

Maybe Vince's mother is angry because she feels she can't go to lunch and shopping because Kate is staying in bed all day.

"I am really sorry that this is impacting your trip, but Kate does not want to be sick. Go about your day and let her sleep in her room today. She just needs some rest."

"I'm not going to leave her alone. I really don't understand why she can't just get dressed and go to lunch and shopping with me."

"When Kate says she is not feeling well, she really is sick. She told me that she has felt something coming on for the last couple of days. Trust me. She just needs twenty-four hours in bed and she will feel better. She can order chicken soup from room service and get some sleep."

"Well, I really think she should go home."

"Is there something else going on that you are not sharing with me?"

"No."

"You can not put her on a plane for twelve hours when she is sick," I say. "And if you send her home because she is sick, it will damage your relationship with her. You won't be able to repair things. I hope you understand that."

"Well, I don't know what to do," Vince's mother says.

I am so confused. I have just told her exactly what she needs to do.

"You don't need to do anything. Kate can take care of herself."

"I will check on her later, and then we will decide what to do."

I feel as if she has not heard a word I have just said. "Very well. I will call my travel agent to find out what Kate's options are."

I am furious. If she truly believes Kate was just

depressed or sad, why on earth would she threaten to send her home? It's unfortunate that Vince's mother is so consumed with grief that it is impossible for her to relate to Kate at all. She is unwilling to provide comfort to her granddaughter while she is ill, and I feel a million miles away. I know Kate can take care of herself in this situation, but now I know she feels even worse because of the conflict with Nana.

My next call is to my sister-in-law. She has no idea what has been happening. She has been with relatives all day. Fortunately, she and I are on the same page about Kate's illness. She offers to speak with Vince's mother and ultimately is able to convince her to not send Kate home.

***

The first draft of my book, *Walking Toward the Light*, has arrived with notes from the editor. I read through all her comments and agree with them. Unfortunately, this will require additional writing to ultimately make it a stronger book. Since returning from Italy, I have felt blocked and unconnected from the universe. I sense my chakras must be out of alignment, so I contact my Reiki therapist for a visit.

I am thrilled that she can fit me into her schedule so quickly. After meditating for a few minutes, I climb up on the table so she can check each chakra. She informs me that my crown, throat and heart chakra are all blocked. I am not surprised. The end of my trip with Vince's mother left me feeling sad and disappointed. As the therapist begins putting her hands on me to heal me, she is able to feel other people's energy around me.

"There is a young man speaking. He says his father abandoned him. He says Sunday dinners are a joke. He does not deserve to be a part of them. A leopard does not change his spots. Just because he is sick does not mean he has changed. Why is everyone rallying around him just because he is sick? Nothing has changed. He is still the same. He never gave me any respect or paid me any attention, so why should I now give him anything because he is dying. He does not deserve my time."

I am lying on a table with my eyes closed, but tears stream down my cheeks. I had been struggling with how to include James in the book. He and Vince had such a strained relationship.

"Does this make any sense to you?" my therapist asks.

"Yes, it does," I whisper.

"This is your son speaking?"

"Yes."

"He is pragmatic. Cut and dry. I see your daughter as being more bendable, like a willow. She is more forgiving," she continues. "Your ex-husband is here."

Perfect. Why is he here?

"I'm just going to say what he is saying to me. I'm not sure what it means, so I will say it exactly as he is saying it," she explains.

Vince comes through with the following messages. "I am sorry that my last act of revenge was towards you. I didn't do what I said I would do for you financially. I was angry and wanted control back in my life. I was angry that I was dying, and it was my last act of control. I acted out of my ego. I acted out of revenge. I didn't want you to have anything. I hurt the one who gave me unconditional love. I lashed out at you. I am sorry."

My reaction surprises me. For a moment I feel light as a feather, like the weight of the world has been lifted from my shoulders. I had always suspected that Vince purposefully did not want to let me stay in his house with the children. But there was part of me that could not believe he had lied to my face about changing how long we could stay in the house.

How could he do something so vicious when I had been so caring?

But I am filled with empathy for this man who could not let go of his ego even at the end, a man who—in the face of absolute love—still chose to inflict pain. I resolved long ago to no longer allow myself to be his victim. I am sad for him that he must live with his choice. I know he made a huge mistake. The reality is that I am the *only* person in his life who saw the real him underneath his ego. I always knew there was a better person beneath all his rage and anger. Unfortunately, he could not let go of his fear so that his heart could soar. I had held out the hope that he would surrender his ego and accept love, but even in the presence of death it was not to be.

"Why are you so critical of me?" There is a long pause before the therapist continues. "You are writing the truth. I was an asshole. I lived my life out of ego. I should have looked deeper. My mother will be upset about the book. Mothers want to protect their children. You are telling the truth even though it is ugly. I will explain to my mother when she gets here. Others will learn from my mistakes. My legacy is that others will learn what not to do. You must share my story."

Of course he would think it is his story.

Even now his ego is still very present. I want to scream. It is not *his* story; it's not even my story. It is our story.

Vince continues speaking through my therapist. "My cancer was a formidable opponent. Too strong for me. I fought from my ego instead of from deeper inside myself. This book will be a way of healing for you and the children. Tell my story so others don't make the same mistakes. Tell the kids I love them very much and I am sorry that I was such a terrible father. Tell Kate I no longer visit her because I am busy living my new life. I have had to learn my lessons again, so I am living another life. Please tell her she does not need me anymore. They are both doing great. You are an amazing mother. Tell them I love them."

The tears now stream down my cheeks. I feel like such a failure. Why couldn't I get him to see that he was surrounded by love and no longer needed to live in fear? I am grateful that he has owned his revenge on me. I didn't want to believe that this man had taken the last piece of love I had given him, taken my heart once again and tossed it aside like trash. It was too unconscionable to imagine. But here he is admitting what he's done.

Our session has come to an end, and I slowly rise from the table. I feel lighter, as if a burden has been lifted from me. I have spent the last few months, since November, trying to make sense of how Vince could lie to my face about the house. Why would he not allow the children to come back to our last family home while they were in college? I have felt guilty since November each time I think Vince did this out of malice, but he has just confirmed what I knew deep down inside. It was a malicious act. I am relaxed as I leave for the thirty-minute drive home.

***

Once home, I put a leash on the dog and take him for his evening walk. With each step, I can feel my feet become heavier and heavier. My shoulders are hunched over and I can barely hold my head up. Exhaustion engulfs me, and I cannot focus. I feel like I am in a fog.

What is wrong with me?

I walk home and I crawl into bed at 5:30 p.m. I have never felt so exhausted. I promptly fall asleep until morning.

When I awake, I feel just as tired and can barely feed and walk the dog before climbing back into bed. I am gripped by exhaustion and depression.

How could he have done that to me?

My mind cannot bear to think about it, and so I sleep.

Depression covers me like a heavy, dark blanket. I wake mid-afternoon.

Why? Why did he do that to me?

I can't bear to be awake because then I am aware of the reality. I roll over, hug my pillow and sleep some more.

I wake the next morning, and the fog has lifted. The word *enough* is swimming in my head. I am angry. After everything I did, he still had to hurt me one last time. This betrayal is much worse than all the lies during our marriage. The wound is deeper this time, because I cared for him and gave him his family back even though he had not changed. Once again, I hear the voices in my head...

Enough.

Enough is enough. I will not spend one more moment trying to rationalize why he did what he did. I moved in with him for James and Kate, so they could have a chance to bond with their father. So they might have a chance to reconcile their relationship with him. My reward is that my children are living life and moving on even though they have lost their father. This is my compensation for caring for Vince. James and Kate have benefited and have learned how to navigate grief and healing. I have committed to sharing *our* story so others will not make the same mistakes. Hopefully our journey will inspire others in some way.

Vince is responsible for his actions. I will not allow myself to be mired in sadness and to feel like a victim again. He has tried to control me for the very last time. His conduct is in the past. I must stop playing the movies of his broken promises in my mind. The theater has closed.

***

Kate's high school graduation is the first major milestone we will celebrate as a family since Vince's passing. James is flying home for the weekend, and Nana will arrive from Philadelphia. My mother will be unable to make the trip, because my father can no longer be left alone. His health is deteriorating each day.

Kate's graduation will be a bittersweet moment for her and for us as a family.

I grab a cup of coffee, head to Kate's room, crawl next to her in bed and enjoy a few quiet moments with her before the chaos begins. "How are you feeling about graduation?" I ask. "Are you nervous, excited, maybe a little sad?"

"I wish I hadn't agreed to go through graduation," she says. "I really don't feel like participating."

I had been the one to encourage her to attend her graduation ceremony even though she graduated in January. High school graduation is a milestone, and I was afraid she would regret not being a part of the celebration.

"Why don't you want to be a part of graduation?

All your friends will be there. I know they are so happy you are home."

"It's not a happy moment for me. Dad is gone, and I am worried that I am going to be sad at the ceremony."

"I understand. You know, every major milestone in your life will be tinged with some sadness now that your father is not with you."

Her eyes fill with tears. "It's just hard knowing he won't be there."

"I know. I really just wanted you to have the option to be part of the graduation ceremony if you wanted. If you would rather skip it, just say the word."

I can't imagine what it must be like for Kate and James to not have their father with them during these important moments.

I think back to James' high school graduation and how we celebrated as a family with both grandmothers and my brother. I remember the tears of pride and joy during the ceremony and how Vince and I had put our own feelings of anger for each other aside for the weekend to celebrate our son's accomplishment. We had no idea at that time that Vince's death was just around the corner.

Unfortunately today, summer weather has created a travel nightmare. Vince's mother's plane was diverted before finally arriving in Chicago four hours late. I know she is exhausted from a long day of travel. I step out of the car to hug her. She is stiff and barely smiles. I load her bag in the back of my car, and we begin the drive home.

"I'm so sorry that you have had such a trying travel day," I say.

"I really don't think I can travel anymore. It's just too exhausting."

"Well, the good news is you have a few years before James' college graduation."

"I plan to be ten feet under by then," she mutters.

Again her desire to be gone is greater than her desire to celebrate her grandchildren's achievements. I can tell that her grief has become her way of life. Depression has settled in. I think it is difficult for her to see us moving on and celebrating life.

The following day is graduation, and we have been invited to the home of one of Kate's friends for a light supper and photos before the ceremony. I am grateful for the invitation. Having other families around will break up the tension. With Vince's mother in the house, there is awkwardness between the four of us. This is the first time she has been in the house since Vince passed, and she is dealing with her own set of memories. We try the best we can to put a happy face on the occasion and celebrate Kate's accomplishment.

We drive to the graduation venue, a large church with enough theater-style seating to accommodate the family members of Kate's graduating class. We decide to sit near the stairs of the first balcony to watch for Kate. The music cues, and a sea of more than nine hundred, red-robed students enters. A lump forms in my throat and tears pool in my eyes as *Pomp & Circumstance* begins to play. I am so very proud of her graduating from high school early and being accepted to a private university. She has matured into such a wonderful young woman. I can't wait to see where she will go from here. I know she must be thinking of Vince and wishing he was here. Tears spill down my cheeks, and I look to my right where no one is seated. I smile warmly knowing that Vince's spirit is standing next to me beaming with pride, as well.

The following day, we head out for a family lunch at one of Kate's favorite Italian restaurants in a neighboring suburb. Vince's mom barely speaks during the meal, and she is expressionless. The conversation is stiff. I am worried for her. Will she be able to work through the sadness? Each time she speaks of Vince, she wells up with tears.

I am grateful the children focus on living each day to the fullest. We have seen the uncertainty of death. There are no guarantees or promises that one will live a long life. We have discussed how important it is to live each day to the best of our ability, not regretting anything and experiencing and embracing everything the day brings.

CHAPTER TEN

JUNE — FATHERS AND DADS

"Any man can be a father
but it takes someone special to be a dad."
— Ann Geddes

I am relishing being together as a family. James will return to school soon, and I am soaking up every minute of time with him and Kate.

James has blossomed at school and flourished under his own autonomy. Before Vince's passing, James was plagued with rage. Vince's constant scrutiny and unrealistic expectations put James in unwinnable situations on a daily basis. Now, he is making his own decisions, charting a course for his life and building confidence with each step.

I have learned to let him make his own choices. As parents, we want our children to have an easier life than we had. We want to spare them all of the hurt and disappointment that our choices may have led to. Our first instinct is to provide direction, and sometimes too much of it. But we have to remember that each one of us is better off because we've made our own individual mistakes and have learned from them. We have to step back and let our children learn the same way. Each time we direct, fix or control a situation for our children, we strip them of the opportunity to grow and build self-confidence.

Before James heads back to school, we attend the high school graduation party for one of Kate's best friends. We have been friends with this family since the girls were just five months old. James was friendly with their middle son when we all lived in the same neighborhood. James has been eschewing family parties for the last few years. I think he felt disconnected from us as a family since he had been away at boarding school. As Kate and I are preparing to leave, James heads up the stairs to the kitchen area.

"I'd like to go with you and Kate to the party." He is dressed in khaki pants, a dress shirt and loafers. He looks so handsome. I am shocked. It has been many years since he attended a family party with us.

"Great. We are leaving in ten minutes," I say.

My heart is full as we make the thirty-minute drive to our friends' house. I have both my children with me. We are a family, happy, healthy and united once again.

***

Unfortunately, on the west coast my father grows sicker with each day. Each morning, I hear the exhaustion in my mother's voice. I barely hear her whispers over the phone. Her energy is depleted and she refuses any help. I encourage her to ask for help from friends and neighbors with things like walking the dog, making dinner, running errands or sitting with my father so she can have a break from the round-the-clock care.

She still continues to work. Every morning she wakes at four, walks the dog, spends time with my father, cooks breakfast for him and dispenses his medication. She prepares a lunch for him and leaves it on the table near the sofa. After breakfast, he falls back to sleep for most of the day.

My mother returns home around 2:30 p.m. to care for my father. She has begun questioning when she should take her leave of absence to stay home with him until he passes. She asks the doctors and hospice nurses for a timeline, but they still have no answer for her. No one can pinpoint the exact day or even week someone will die. They've ordered a medical bed to assist my father with sitting up. I try to support my mother by sharing my experiences of this time with Vince, but the end is different for everyone, and it's different for each caregiver, too.

At night, my father has dreams and visions of people and animals in the house. A full night of sleep has eluded my mother for months. She is run down, and she's having a hard time remaining patient with my father. During the night, the toxins build in his brain. I remember this time well with Vince.

"I know it's easy to become frustrated and short," I say. "You are sleep deprived and he is difficult to manage at night. He wants to get out of bed and do things that are not safe to do in his condition. But take a deep breath and be patient. I used to think of Vince as a child during this time. You would never yell at a child. So treat him with the care and patience you would a kid. You would feel horrible if your last words to him where harsh."

She thanks me for sharing my experiences, but she needs more than just my emotional support.

I make the decision to fly to California in a week, which will be the Monday after Father's Day. This news seems to lift my mother's spirit if only for a moment.

Tuesday, hospice begins visiting my father, providing end-of-life care to keep him comfortable and pain free. My mother has taken the day off so she can be there when the nurse comes to check my father. He is in good spirits and jokes with the nurse. He is having some discomfort, so she prescribes morphine. Patients often don't want to take morphine because it makes it feel like the end to them. He shares his concern with the nurse that he will become addicted to the morphine. The reality is that he will probably pass within the next couple of weeks, which makes addiction a non-issue.

On Wednesday morning I speak with my mother. Although still depleted of energy, she sounds in much better spirits. She tells me that the morphine energized my father, so they walked around the park—something my father has not done in a long time. My father was excited that he felt so good and told my mother that he should have begun taking morphine earlier if it was going to help him feel so good.

"That's great," I say.

I can hear the hope in her voice. I can't bear to tell her that this is my father's burst of energy. It is very common for patients at the end of life to have a burst of energy where they seem to rally and bounce back. No one can predict when it will occur or how long it will last. It can last a few minutes, a few hours or a few days. In Vince's case, it was a few days.

When I speak with my mother Thursday morning, everything has changed. Her voice cracks as she talks. My father had a very tough night. He needed to use the bathroom and he was able to walk there but did not have the strength to walk back to his bed. I remember what this was like when Vince no longer had the energy to walk to the bathroom. She explains that she had him sit in his walker that has wheels and she tried to push him back to his bed. It took every last bit of strength she had to push and pull him back into bed.

"I think I should call work and tell them that I am going to start my vacation," she says. "I think it is time for me to stay home with your father."

"That's a great idea. I will be there on Monday to help you."

"Okay. I'm fine really."

I can tell she needs help earlier than Monday, so I hang up the phone and call the airlines to make arrangements to fly in Saturday morning.

Kate's future college roommate will be flying in from Jackson, Mississippi, so that the girls can get to know each other before school begins. My plan was to spend the weekend with them, but at least I will get to meet Kate's roommate before I head to California.

I call my mother back. "I just changed my travel plans. I am flying in Saturday; that way I can be there for Father's Day."

I am concerned about leaving Kate for her first Father's Day without Vince, but her roommate will be with her, and they are planning to attend a concert on Sunday in Chicago.

"You don't have to do that. I know Kate's roommate is in town."

"They are happy that I am leaving them for the weekend. They don't need me hovering over them. I'll be there on Saturday."

I speak with my mother later in the afternoon on Thursday. My father had spent the entire day in bed, and when hospice came to visit, the decision was made to stop giving him medications.

"He asked me why he doesn't have to take his pills," my mom tells me. "I couldn't bear to tell him that his body is giving up."

My heart aches to hear this news.

"He asked me if he is dying," she continues. "I said, 'yes.'"

I hear the exhaustion and fear in my mother's voice.

I had warned her that the day would come when she would be chained to the house unable to even leave the room. There comes a point near the end when you can no longer leave your patient alone for even a minute. Vince would often try to get up, which would have been completely unsafe. He was so weak that his legs could not support his body. He was unable to articulate what he wanted, and I would have to convince him to lie back in bed. This occurred every two hours at night the last week of his life. It was exhausting, and I know my mother has begun dealing with this phase.

On Friday, I talk to my mother again. She slept on the sofa to be near my father in his hospital bed, but has barely slept at all. She tells me that at one point in the night, he instructed my mother to help him gather up the chickens.

I recall the last week of Vince's life when he would think he was in a meeting and ask me if I had the presentation ready to go and if I had confirmed that everyone would be there. My advice to my mother has been to go with the conversation. It is more unsettling for the person if you try to bring them back to reality. In Vince's case, I went along with the story. I assured him that I confirmed the meeting and that the presentation was ready. At one point, he told me he did not recognize anyone in the room, and I assured him that they would introduce themselves. Who knows what he was seeing at the time? I imagined he was reliving a business meeting or maybe he was meeting some of the angels who would escort him from this life.

I can tell my mother is feeling alone and helpless. Just nine months earlier, I had stood in the exact same place. The moment you become housebound—afraid to leave, waiting for the end and not knowing when it will be—you feel an immense amount of stress and pressure.

"Hang in there, Mom. I will be there tomorrow afternoon."

My next call is to my brother. I leave him a voicemail asking him if he can drive down in the evening to stay with mom until I arrive Saturday.

My father has been hospitalized numerous times over the past year, and, each time, my brother has dropped everything to be there with my parents. Most of the time, my father is released rather quickly. So it is a surprise to my brother that dad is doing so badly.

My brother returns my call, and he asks if I think he should take the day off and go down to my parent's house. I explain that Mom is pretty tired and she needs a break.

"What would you do if you were here?" he asks. "Is it that bad?"

"I would take the day off. I'm not sure how bad it is. I just know Mom needs some support right now and she is refusing to ask for help."

"I'll head down after I pack a bag."

I call my mother back to inform her that my brother will be coming down in a couple of hours to spend the night with her. She is angry with me for calling him because she does not want him taking a day off to help her.

"I do not need help."

"I know you don't, but it would make us feel better if he was there until I can get there. I know you have everything covered."

***

Several hours later, I am attending a lunch when my phone vibrates. I look down to see a picture of my brother. I immediately answer his call.

"Hey, how's it going?"

"You need to come now."

My stomach sinks. I know my brother would not tell me to come if it was not dire.

"Okay. I'm leaving my lunch now. I will get on the next flight."

My hands are shaking and my heart is racing as I say my goodbyes and begin the drive home. Of course it is a Friday afternoon and there is lots of traffic, so the trip home takes almost an hour. I call the airline to rebook my ticket. Unfortunately, most of the Friday evening flights are sold out, but I have a wonderful customer service agent who sympathizes with my predicament and remains on the phone with me until she is able to secure a seat for me on the 8 p.m. flight, landing at 10 p.m. in San Francisco. My mind is swimming with tasks I need to complete and phone calls I need to make before I can leave.

I quickly pack my carry-on suitcase with a few casual items and toiletries, so I will not have to wait for my luggage when I arrive. My mother and I have already spoken about the funeral arrangements for my father. He will be cremated, and she will host a memorial service a week or so after his passing, so I will not need to pack funeral clothing.

***

I slip into my window seat and acknowledge my seatmate. He nods and quickly puts his headphones in his ears. I breathe a deep sigh of relief. I am grateful he seems just as uninterested in speaking with me as I am with him. My father is dying and I just want to be quiet right now. I have a déjà vu moment. I feel as if I have stood in this place once before. Allowing someone to die at home is a grueling and selfless act. My role this time will be to help my mother let my father go and give my father permission to leave. My brother and I will watch over my mother. I am sad knowing my father will pass this weekend. Memories of Vince's passing come rushing in.

The flight seems unusually long this evening. I listen to music and stare out the window. My thoughts turn to my mother. I am concerned how she will handle losing her partner, husband and best friend of fifty years. They married at such a young age. She will be forced to build a life for herself once he is gone.

As the plane lands in San Francisco, I switch on my phone to see a text from my brother asking if I have landed. I text back and then cue the car service that I will be ready shortly. I am hoping I don't have to wait too long for my car to pick me up. I am anxious to get to my parents' house. Suddenly, my phone vibrates. It is my brother calling.

I am still on the airplane when I answer. "Hey, everything okay?"

There is a brief moment of silence.

"Hey, sis, he passed at 10 o'clock."

"What?"

I can barely believe it.

"He passed, Karen."

"All right. I will be there as soon as I can."

My eyes brim with tears. It never occurred to me that I would not make it in time to see him. He was lucid just twenty-four hours ago. I look out the window, and the tears begin to roll down my cheeks. Guilt washes over me. I can't believe I did not make it in time to say goodbye. I knew the last time we saw each other that it was the last time I would probably see him. I always figured I would get a call in Chicago that he had passed and would then fly to California. But I never imagined I'd be trying to get there to see him and not make it. I remind myself that everything happens for a reason and that I was not meant to be there. But I should have been there for my mother.

***

The car ride to my parents' seems to take an eternity. I weep softly in the backseat, unbeknownst to the driver. He has no idea what is happening. As I pull into my parents' community, I text my brother. When the car pulls up to the house, he and my mother are waiting outside. I immediately step out of the car and hug my mother.

"I'm so sorry I was not here."

"It's okay," she says. "You're here now. We have not called the funeral home. We were waiting for you to get here."

I am not surprised to find my mother very composed and stoic. Despite the weariness and uncertainty that have been her constant companions for the past few months, she is the strongest woman I know.

The driver removes my luggage from the trunk and tells me to have a nice visit. All three of us smile as he gets in the car. The poor guy had no idea what type of visit he was driving me to.

As I walk into the house, I see my father lying in his hospital bed. He looks much different than Vince did when he passed. All the blood has drained from my father's face. Even his large red birthmark has vanished. He looks peaceful but very pale. I reach down to hold his hand, and it is cold. He is gone. I bend down to kiss his cheek.

"Sorry I didn't make it, Dad."

"He knows you tried to make it," my mom says.

Throughout the evening, my father had been mostly sleeping, but he would wake occasionally to say something. My brother had kept him updated on my progress throughout the night. He was tracking my flight with an app on his phone and periodically showed my father where my plane was. As the night wore on, my father became different when he woke up. He did not seem like himself. At one point, he asked my mother if he had died.

She shook her head.

But he looked at her with a childlike expression.

"Am I dying?" he asked.

"Yes," she said.

I can only imagine the sadness and strength my mother had at that very moment. Her husband of fifty years was dying.

"I want you to know that I am so sorry for anything I ever said or did that hurt you," he said.

Two of my father's sisters have been with my mother and brother all day and night. None of us knew that today would be the day my father would pass. His sisters happened to come by to visit him and see if my mother needed any help. Their help and emotional support was priceless.

My brother calls the funeral home and asks that they pick up my father's body. We will spend the next couple of hours sitting with my father in the living room as my family recounts the day and evening to me. I am grateful that my father has passed so peacefully. I am thankful that my mother's role as caretaker is done. The stress was beginning to take a toll on her emotionally and physically.

At 1 a.m., the funeral home arrives to remove my father's body. From my experiences with Vince I know that they recommend the family not watch as they put the body in the transport bag. The body is heavy, and it can be very unsettling to watch as people you don't know jostle about your loved one's remains. I suggest my mother and brother go into the other room while they put my father's body in the bag. I will stay. I feel like it is my role now to step in and help facilitate what needs to be done. My brother and mother have had a long and emotionally draining day. As they begin preparing to remove my father, my aunt becomes agitated at how they are handling his body. This is the reason family should not watch this process. I send her into the bedroom with my mother and brother so the men can do their job. They strap my father's body to a gurney and remove him from the house.

I remember when they removed Vince's body from the house. I watched them bring him down the stairs and slowly wheel him out the front door. They were so respectful with their handling of Vince's body.

My father's youngest sister stands on the front porch with me as they load my father's body into the van. I feel the same sense of responsibility now, as I did with Vince, to watch the van drive away with my father.

"He was a great man and father," I say.

"Yes, he was."

My mother and I have always discussed how she wants to move forward after my father's death. She does not want to become a depressed, sad person living in the past, mired in grief. It is now time to celebrate my father's life and not look back at regrets. There is a very overused quote, "any man can be a father but it takes a special man to be a dad." Vince was a father and never figured out how to be a dad. However, my father was my dad. There were years where he made time for us, and we had the chance to learn and experience life from his point of view. There were other times when he was busy building his business and launching his career as a contractor. I choose now to remember my "dad," the man who broke family molds to not just be a father, but to be a dad.

The minute grieving begins, you have the opportunity to choose to celebrate life or live in loss. Death is inevitable and living in loss is not what my father would want. He would want us to celebrate his life, our life together, and find a way to find joy and happiness in life without him.

I walk into my mother's room to let her know that dad is gone. We bid our goodbyes to my aunts. They have been so helpful, and it is time now for everyone to sleep. My mother and brother are exhausted, and frankly, so am I. Sleep comes swiftly, and I dream of my father.

***

The next morning, we wake up and begin removing any memories of my father's illness, such as medications and hospital supplies. We push the hospital bed into the dining room. My advice is to remove all the medical equipment, medications and items that will remind you of the person's illness as soon as possible. This allows the family to embrace living again and removes the reminders of how hard the last few days, weeks or months have been. My mother had always wanted the TV in the living room to be in a different spot. I suggest to my brother we move it for her. This requires my brother crawling under the house to move the cable line, but he attacks the project with bravery. We decide we can't wait until the following week for all the hospital equipment to be removed, so we dismantle the bed, oxygen tanks, chairs and walkers and place them in the garage. My mom is pleased to have the house look like a home again rather than a hospital facility. This is key to my mother being able to move forward without my father.

Some people may not agree with removing items from the house so quickly, but I have a theory. In the first couple of days after someone has passed, you are in shock. You are numb, so this is the best time to remove things. You are so numb that you forget your attachments to these material things. Once the fog lifts, you are ready to start grieving, and you can begin the process in a much healthier manner if the signs of illness have been removed. If you wait until later to remove these items, you might feel an unhealthy attachment to them, and the task may prove difficult.

Later in the afternoon, neighbors and family stop by to pay their respects. My father was somewhat of an icon in the community where my parents live. That evening, the three of us decide to stay in and reminisce about Dad over cocktails. It is a fun evening filled with lots of laughter, and I'm pretty sure my father is there with us laughing all night long.

***

The next day, my brother and I begin planning my father's memorial service. He is being cremated, and we will host a small service for immediate family and close friends at my parents' community clubhouse. My father wanted us to celebrate his life and accomplishments. He did not want a somber occasion filled with tears. My brother and I plan a memorial celebration that honors his wishes. My mother also has some requests, as well, and my brother and I hold firm to her requirements.

We have spent the last few days sending invitations, calling friends, hiring a caterer and working on all the various details of the memorial service. On Wednesday, my brother and I decide it is a good idea to stagger our departures. He leaves on Thursday to return to work for the following week. I will leave Saturday to return to Chicago. The memorial service will be the following Saturday. I plan to fly back to California on Thursday with James and Kate. This is the first death in the family since James and Kate lost their father. I know this may be a difficult occasion for them.

***

The kids and I arrive back in San Francisco the following Thursday. We are staying at a hotel near my mother's house, and my brother is staying with my mother. Even though it is a somber time, we are all very excited to be together. James and Kate are a huge help executing all of our plans from the previous week. My brother and James even move my parents' flat screen TV to the clubhouse so we can play a DVD of my father's life that my brother has made.

The day of the memorial service we are all busy in the morning with final preparations. The boys set up the TV and make sure the audio system works properly. Kate and I decorate the tables with clay pots filled with yellow mums, a nod to my father's southern roots. The caterer arrives to set up a light luncheon with sandwiches and salads.

I am pleased when James checks in with my brother to see how he is feeling about the day. James shares his own personal experience of attending Vince's funeral and offers his emotional support. James is the rock today for both my brother and me. At several points he steps in to take over tasks.

We wanted the memorial service to not only be a remembrance of my father but also a party honoring his life. My father always wore dark sunglasses everywhere he went, whether he was indoors or outdoors. Everyone knew him for his dark sunglasses. As a way to honor my father, we purchased a pair of sunglasses for each attendee at the service and display them on the tables where guests will be seated. The room looks bright, fun and festive, and I am sure my father would approve.

We all dress in somber colors for the afternoon. My brother heads to the clubhouse first in case any guests arrive early. I go next to check on the caterer, and James and Kate arrive shortly after. When the kids show up, James tells me that Mimi is back at the house crying. He takes over handling the caterer so that I can rush home.

I find my mom curled up on the sofa. "I know today will be hard for you," I say. "At any point if you need anything, you let me know. Can I help you get ready?"

She shakes her head no and excuses herself to get dressed for the service. My mother does not like to cry in front of people, so I am cautious to give her space today. A few minutes before the start of the memorial, I drive my mother down to the clubhouse. Some guests have already arrived, and my mother is grateful for the distraction.

The memorial is a lovely tribute to my father. My brother's DVD showcases all my father's accomplishments and the things he was most proud of. My brother and I take turns talking about my father, sharing his accomplishments and cracking a few jokes along the way. My mother stands at the end to thank everyone for coming. She is poised and eloquent. It is a simple celebration—just as my mother wanted. She is pleased and relieved. As we all depart the following day, she is left to begin building a life without my father.

CHAPTER ELEVEN

JULY — MEMENTOS

"The most important things in life are not things."
— Unknown

I am finally ready to finish moving into Vince's home. I hire movers to move the last of our belongings from our previous house out of storage. It has been eighteen months since the children and I moved into Vince's home. It is time to combine the two households—even though I will need to move again in November of 2014.

I meet the movers at our storage facility. They quickly pack up all the belongings and bring them to our home. The garage will be the unpacking area for the next several weeks. A sea of boxes, bins and sporting equipment fills the space. I stand amongst the boxes, lips trembling. This is our life, our history, our mementos. I am so tired of packing and unpacking.

My anger for Vince wells up inside of me.

Why couldn't he just do one nice thing for me? Why

couldn't he let the children and me stay just a few more years until they were done with college?

I am so angry and disappointed at his betrayal. But I realize I am only hurting myself. He is gone and he cannot feel my anger. I must remember why I moved in with Vince. James and Kate had the opportunity to spend time with their father, and they have been able to grieve and move on with their lives. I take a deep breath and open up a box.

It takes me weeks to unpack. I spend the evenings sorting through each box, sometimes giggling at the memorabilia from our past. Other times I cry, lamenting that the years have gone by far too quickly for me. There are space constraints in Vince's home, so I choose the most important keepsakes for James and Kate and place them in their designated bins. There is not enough room for all of my linens and housewares, so I decide to have another garage sale. These were my favorite items that I saved from our previous house, but there is no room for them here. These are just material things anyway. My happiness lies in my life and who I am, not in the things I own.

***

The very next weekend I have my last garage sale. The final pieces of my previous life of materialism and affluence will be sold today. By two, I have sold everything except a small box of items, which I will donate to a charity. I survey the empty garage and I am content and filled with a peace that I have not known in a very long time. I recall the last eighteen months, and it is hard to fathom all that has happened. I think of my mother, who will soon begin the process of clearing out my father's belongings.

***

Now it is time to begin preparing Kate for her move to college in August. We fly to Dallas the following week to attend orientation. Her roommate and her family will also be in Dallas. We all decide to stay at the same hotel. The four-day trip is filled with orientation, meetings with counselors, tours of the campus and dorms. Kate and her roommate are thrilled that they are able to secure housing in their first choice dorm. It is hard to believe that she will leave for school in just five weeks.

***

James is attending his last session of summer school in Cincinnati. He is excited to return home in a couple of weeks for the balance of the summer. James has kept several of his father's items to remember him by. His golf clubs stand in the corner of the basement family room as a reminder of Vince's love of golf. James golfs as a lefty so he cannot play with Vince's clubs, but he derives some peace in knowing these were his father's.

James has also decided to keep Vince's desk and chair. It is a traditional desk with black leather inlays in the top. The chair is tufted, navy blue leather. James grew up watching Vince work at this desk, a fitting reminder of Vince's success. I have no doubt James will find his own success.

Moving in the last of our belongings and selling off what does not fit into Vince's house has also allowed us to grieve further. We hastily moved from our previous home and packed up so quickly that we were not able to make decisions about what to keep. With everything in its place, we feel the sense of peace that comes with settling in. We have finally made Vince's house our home.

CHAPTER TWELVE

AUGUST — I WISH DAD WERE HERE

*"If there comes a day when we can't be together,
keep me in your heart, I will stay there forever."*
— A. A. Milne (author of the Winnie the Pooh Books)

I am always surprised how ill prepared I am for the month of August. When the children were in grade school, the summer months lulled me into a false sense of calm. The days were long, and there were no after school activities or homework. However, school would always begin the third week of August, and I always underestimated how much time, effort and energy was required to start up again.

Preparing your children for college is no different. These are young adults who are preparing to live on their own. They are able to drive and make their own decisions, so one would think it would be easier, but it's not.

The month begins with James moving into a new apartment with one of his roommates from last year. He is better prepared this year and has found a nicer place closer to campus. He insisted on negotiating the lease himself and handling all the necessary deposits and signatures. He is growing up.

James and I make the drive to Cincinnati to move his stuff out of his old apartment and into a new one. We arrive at dusk, check into our hotel and eat a quick dinner. I have never had the opportunity to tour the campus, so James suggests that we walk around. It is dark, and all the buildings are lit. The campus is beautiful at night. I am in awe of the architecture with old buildings mixed in with contemporary structures. It is a sprawling, closed campus, and James knows the names of each building. He beams with confidence as we explore the school.

We continue to walk around the campus, and I am aware of someone walking just behind me over my right shoulder. I turn around, but no one is there. I walk a few more steps forward and am suddenly aware that I feel Vince's spirit near me. He is touring the campus with us. Vince never had the opportunity to visit James' college or to help him move to school. He was too sick to make the trip. Sadly, he would die just three weeks after James left for Ohio. I hope he sees how confident, strong and determined James has become.

I drop James back at his apartment for the evening. He and his roommate need to clean up the place before they move out the following morning. I head back to the hotel for a peaceful night's sleep. The next morning James calls and asks me to pick up a few items on my way to their apartment. He assures me things are under control with the clean up.

I arrive at their apartment to find his roommate's mother scouring the kitchen. The place looks like a war zone, and I can tell she has been cleaning all morning. I feel horrible I did not arrive earlier and immediately jump in to help scrub. By one, we are done and have the boxes loaded into our SUVs. The boys cannot pick up the keys to their new apartment until two, so I invite his roommate and his mother to have lunch at our hotel. She and I are exhausted. We promise ourselves that we will never clean another apartment again. Boys are such slobs. Their version of clean and a mother's version of clean are on opposite sides of a spectrum.

We pull up to the new apartment. It is a great location, just a few short blocks from campus. It is a secure complex, and no one can enter the property without a security code.

The boys bound up the steps two at a time. I gather a few items from the trunk and head toward the stairs.

I find James standing on the landing looking back at me sheepishly. "We have a problem."

"I'm not cleaning another apartment today," I yell, thinking the previous tenants left a mess.

"You should probably come up and look," he says.

I walk into the apartment, which has granite counters and beautiful hardwood floors but no furniture.

"I didn't realize it would not be furnished. My last apartment was."

"What did the lease say?" I ask.

"I don't know," he says with a shrug and a grin.

"Well you are locked into the lease. There is nothing we can do about it now. Finish unloading the car while I think for a minute."

His roommate's mother and I shake our heads in disbelief. We smile at each other. What an easy mistake to make, one James will never make again. His roommate's mother offers to send several pieces of spare furniture from their home. Fortunately, they live nearby. James and I make the trek to IKEA, the best place to purchase affordable college items.

We spend the next two hours selecting a sofa, bar stools, a bed, chest, desk, chairs, area rug and TV stand. James is receiving an excellent first-hand education about purchasing furniture. We arrange to have the items delivered and assembled, but they will not arrive until mid-week. The boys will need to make do on a couple of air mattresses for a few nights. James had originally planned to come back to Chicago with me, but now he will have to stay for the delivery of all his stuff.

***

Just two weeks later, Kate is off to college. She and I fly to Mississippi, where we will join her roommate's family at their home. We will then caravan to Dallas, which is only a five-hour drive. This allows us to ship all Kate's belongings to

Jackson instead of having to coordinate shipping with the school. Kate's roommate will be bringing her SUV to school, and I have rented an SUV in Jackson. After we move the girls into their dorm room, I will make the drive back to Jackson with Kate's roommate's mom and then return to Chicago.

I am excited for Kate to begin her college career even though it means she will be a plane ride away. She is quiet the morning of move-in. I secretly wonder if she is nervous about school. We have arranged through the school to hire two young men to help carry in all the boxes and suitcases from our vehicles. The day is incredibly hot and very humid. We decide to tag team. Kate's roommate's mother stays in the dorm room helping the girls set things up. I stay with the vehicles until they are completely unloaded and then head upstairs.

Kate is stressed and complaining about the size of the room and closet. Every mother who has moved a daughter into a dorm room knows exactly what I am talking about. She is feeling overwhelmed and begins to take it out on me. The girls still need a few items for their room, so the moms decide to make a Target run. We run through the store like crazy women buying a printer and additional items. On the way back to the dorm, we call the girls and offer to pick up lunch. When we arrive back, they've both showered and freshened up.

We sit on the floor and eat lunch together. I try to make conversation with Kate, but she has shut down. I've never really seen her this way. I am trying very hard not to take it personally, but I am a little sad. I had this idyllic vision of mother and daughter chatting excitedly about how to organize her room and then hugging goodbye through tears at the end.

We can hear music playing from outside, and freshmen are beginning to mill around the dorm. The girls are ready for us to go. Kate can barely look at me, and I know she does not want to say goodbye. Maybe she is worried that I will cry. A large lump forms in my throat, and I awkwardly give Kate a hug. I am envious as her roommate tightly embraces her mother.

"Bye," Kate says. She quickly turns her back to me.

I pat her shoulder. "Have a great time and see you parents' weekend."

The lump is growing in my throat and tears begin to fill my eyes. I implore myself not to cry, but the minute I reach the car, the tears spill from my eyes. My baby is on her own. The glaring reality is that I'm not ready to be on *my* own just yet. I am grateful to share the ride back to Jackson with Kate's roommate's mother. We get along very well and enjoy each other's company. She has graciously extended an invitation for me to spend the night at her home.

***

The next morning I wake early to a text from Kate. It's an apology for our awkward goodbye. She is excited and looking forward to the start of school on Monday. I am happy to hear she is settled and having fun.

I head to the airport in Jackson and wait for my flight to board. It is a short flight back to Chicago, and as we begin our descent I feel lost. I am officially an empty nester, living all alone. I wonder where all the years went. It was a blur. Being a mom has always been my first priority, but now I realize my role has changed. I now have a void to fill.

I find myself alone. Since moving in with Vince in 2011, I have not dated. I did not date out of respect for our children and our living situation. After Vince passed, I was consumed with making sure the kids were okay. I also needed to rebuild my company. I have wonderful friends and neighbors, but they have their own families and are busy with their spouses. Chicago no longer feels like my home.

***

I fly to California at the end of the month to spend some quality time with my mother. I plan to spend a couple of weeks with her, and I am grateful for the distraction. We work on making her house feel like home for her now that my father is gone. I take time to reconnect with a few friends from high school and my cousins. As I drive around, I wonder why I never considered moving back to California.

Suddenly the date November 2014 registers in my consciousness, the date I must vacate Vince's house. No matter where I move to in Chicago, it will never feel like home for James and Kate.

So why am I staying there? Maybe it's time for a fresh start. Maybe it's time for me to go home.

It is a sunny day, and I am driving down El Camino Real in Menlo Park when I make the official decision to move back to California.

Thank you, Vince, for your last act of revenge. Lemonade out of lemons.

EPILOGUE

"You will know you made the right decision when you pick
the hardest and most painful choice
but your heart is at peace."

Today is June 15, 2014 (Father's Day) and I am completing the first draft of my second book. It has been a year since my father's passing and almost two years since Vince's passing. The past year has been one of growth and bonding.

My mother continues to navigate life without my father. I am so incredibly proud of her. We were speaking about grief the other day, and she said, "Losing someone you love leaves a gaping hole in your heart. Each day the hole shrinks a little bit, becoming smaller and smaller over time, but never totally going away."

I agree.

My mother chooses to live life to the fullest rather than wallowing in sorrow. Some days are harder than others, but she knows tomorrow the hole will be just a bit smaller and a little less painful. She is an inspiration.

James and I have a new bond. Gone are the days when we could barely talk. We have both grown through our losses. The pain has made us both stronger and brought us closer together. He continues to flourish at college, and now plans for his career and dreams of his future fill his head. He has grown into an amazing young man, and I am incredibly proud of him. He has become a full-time resident of Ohio but will always be a Chicago boy at heart.

Kate has completed her first year of college and is thriving at school in Texas, as well. She continues to be an excellent student but still makes time to live life, enjoy friends and have fun. She has begun to miss her father in different ways than James does. She can no longer remember what his voice sounds like. She is distressed that she is beginning to lose her memories of him. I encourage parents who will leave children behind, to record a video so whenever your child feels the need to connect with you even though you are gone, he or she can play the video and remember your voice.

Both James and Kate have their moments where they are sad or miss their father. But they have both chosen to move on with their lives. I'm sure they think of Vince often and hope that he is proud of them and their choices. I know he must be. There is a quote, "Time heals all wounds." I'm not sure James and Kate will ever feel fully healed, but like my mother says, the hole in their hearts will become a little smaller each day.

And me, I am preparing for my move back to California, where I grew up. It has not been an easy decision to leave Chicago, but I feel it is time to move on. It is time for me to build a life of my own now that my children are grown. It is time for a fresh start, a new beginning. Ironically, Vince has made this move possible. Had I not had the pressure of having to move in November 2014, I don't think I would have considered moving back to California.

I am grateful for all my experiences, which have provided me with a new career as an author and speaker. California is the perfect place to launch myself. I hope to use my experiences with forgiveness, healing and grief to inspire others to live the best life possible.

I have begun hosting seminars and workshops, sharing my experiences of forgiveness and leading people to their own forgiveness. I am passionate about inspiring people to live more fulfilling lives through forgiveness, healing and processing grief.

Wish me luck, and stay tuned for book three of the "Walking Beyond Series." To download an excerpt from *Walking on Eggshells* visit www.walkingbeyond.com. And also watch for *FORGIVENESS is a Cookie*, my first cookbook. Turn the pages for a few recipes.

ACKNOWLEDGEMENTS

Writing a book that shares such intimate stories and insights has truly been a labor of love. Over the past two years, there are many people who have helped me through the writing and healing process. I am blessed to have such amazing people in my life.

Audra Wilke, thank you for being an amazing business coach. You always hold me accountable and keep me focused throughout the writing process. (www.audrawilke.com)

Betsy Curran, my dear friend of thirty-two years, thank you for being the last set of eyes to proof each of my books. You have a remarkable ability to catch even the tiniest of typos.

Debbie Obradovich, thank you for keeping my chakras aligned and helping me heal my spirit. Your ability to read energy has helped me immensely in my writing process. (reikienergy8@gmail.com)

Evelyn and Henry Laxgang, my dear neighbors, thank you for always being there with a home-cooked meal and glass of wine when I return from traveling to speaking engagements about forgiveness.

Ginny Conners, thank you for dressing me in the most current fashions and making sure I look fabulous at all of my book signings and workshops. (www.ginnyconners.cabionline.com)

Jennifer Chesak, my amazing editor, thank you for working so diligently to edit my books. Your guidance and notes help me make sure the stories are honest, meaningful and ready for the world. (www.wanderinginthewordspress.com).

Lisa Hagenbuch, thank you for expanding my awareness of natal charts and the power of planetary energy in our lives. Through your energy counseling, you opened up my entire world immediately. I see how the past, the present and the future are all aligning to create my life today. (www.integrativediscoveries.com)

Melissa Giovagnoli Wilson, thank you for your wisdom and guidance in writing and publishing my first book. Your workshop outlining the self-publishing process launched me as an author and speaker. (www.networlding.com)

Monica Lee, thank you for your insights regarding the Association of Personal Historians, a great group of professionals ready to help anyone capture his or her personal story and leave a legacy. (www.personalhistorians.org)

Marilyn Todd, my very brave mother, thank you for sharing your story of Dad's passing and your grief so others might be better prepared to navigate such a difficult time.

Margo Kampsen, thank you for being Murphy's surrogate dog mother when I travel.

Penny Holland and Peggy Claire, my adopted sisters, thank you for encouraging me to be brave enough to share my story with the world.

Tatlin, my amazing cover designer, thank your for transforming my visions into incredible covers that evoke emotion. (www.tatlin.net)

Vicki MacKinnon, thank you for the gift of red shoes to remind me that I have always had the power to inspire others. I just needed to step into my shoes.

A sneak peek…

FORGIVENESS is a Cookie: Recipes from the Heart

If you have read *Walking Toward the Light*, you know that while caring for Vince, I channeled my passion for cooking to plant the seeds of forgiveness in my heart. The more I cooked, the more forgiveness took root.

I have always enjoyed cooking for my family, and now as the kids are away at college, I often host dinners prepared with fresh organic ingredients for my friends. I love layering simple flavors to create an intricate meal prepared with love and gratitude.

We cook in order to feed and nurture our bodies and those of our families. Cooking a healthy meal requires dedication, patience and intention. In my journey over the past two years, I found great comfort in the positive feelings I experienced when I stood in the kitchen chopping, stirring and mixing ingredients in the name of nourishing my loved ones.

I am so excited to share my passion for food with you in my first cookbook, which will be available in 2016. Until then, here are two of my favorite recipes filled with healthy ingredients and lots of love:

Avocado, Beet, Orange Salad
(serves 3 to 4)

Ingredients:

3 medium size beets, roasted and cut into small pieces (see roasting instructions below)

1/3 cup pistachios, shelled and oven roasted (see roasting instructions below)

1 avocado, chopped

1 navel orange, peeled, sliced and cut into sections

2 tablespoons fresh-squeezed juice from an orange

1 tablespoon walnut oil

Freshly ground sea salt to taste

Preheat oven to 400 degrees. Trim the beets by cutting off the bottoms and removing the stems and greens from the top. Scrub the beets and place in aluminum foil. Smaller beets can be wrapped together. Larger beets should be wrapped individually. Place beets on a cookie sheet in case beet juices leak. Bake for 50 to 60 minutes (until you are able to pierce the beets with a fork). Let cool and then slide skins off using a paper towel to prevent your hands from staining. Skins should slide off easily. Quarter beets and cut into bite-size pieces.

Roast pistachios on a cookie sheet at 350 degrees for 5 minutes. Set aside to cool.

Combine pieces of beets, avocado and navel orange in a large bowl. In a smaller bowl, whisk together the fresh-squeezed orange juice and walnut oil. Add the oil mixture to the ingredients above and toss. Add pistachios and toss once more. Add salt to taste.

Mushroom Risotto
(serves 3 to 4)

Ingredients:
½ Vidalia onion, finely chopped
1 8-ounce package (12 to 15 medium size) "baby bella" or dark colored mushrooms, chopped
4 cups organic, low-sodium chicken broth
2 tablespoons olive oil
1½ cups uncooked Arborio rice
½ cup good quality pinot grigio or other white wine
1 teaspoon sea salt
1 teaspoon white truffle oil
2 tablespoons fresh parsley, chopped
1/3 cup Parmesan cheese, freshly grated
Ground pepper to taste

Chop onions and mushrooms and set aside in separate bowls. Place the chicken broth in a small saucepan and warm. Keep chicken broth on low heat during the cooking process.

Heat olive oil on medium-high in a 3-quart saucepan. Add onion and cook until the onions are translucent (about 3 minutes). Add mushrooms and sauté for 3 to 5 minutes, until brown and moisture is released into the pan.

Turn heat to low. Add Arborio rice and stir continuously to coat with olive oil. Cook for 2 minutes to release the starch from the rice. Add ½ cup of white wine to mixture. Stir continuously until the wine is absorbed by the rice.

Add ½ cup of chicken broth and continue stirring until rice has absorbed the broth. Repeat until all broth has been absorbed. This process will take approximately 25 to 30 minutes. After the last ½ cup of broth has been absorbed, the rice should be slightly *al dente*.

Remove rice from heat. Stir in sea salt, chopped parsley and truffle oil. Place rice in a serving bowl and sprinkle with grated Parmesan cheese and freshly ground pepper to taste.

www.ingramcontent.com/pod-product-compliance
Lightning Source LLC
Chambersburg PA
CBHW072006040426

42447CB00009B/1513